HEALING PRIESTHOOD

Helen –
A little light reading
during those dark
Winter evenings in Oxford.

Ed

HEALING
PRIESTHOOD

WOMEN'S VOICES
WORLDWIDE

~

Edited by
ANGELA PERKINS and VERENA WRIGHT

DARTON·LONGMAN + TODD

First published in 2003 by
Darton, Longman and Todd Ltd
1 Spencer Court
140–142 Wandsworth High Street
London SW18 4JJ

ISBN 0–232–52506–4

A catalogue record for this book is available from the British Library.

Set in 10.75/13pt Baskerville
Designed and produced by Sandie Boccacci
using QuarkXPress on an Apple PowerMac
Printed and bound in Great Britain by
Page Bros, Norwich, Norfolk

CONTENTS

CONTENTS

ACKNOWLEDGEMENTS

We would like to thank Freda Lambert and Mary Brogan (past Presidents), appointed by the NBCW Executive to approve the final copy, for their advice and assistance. We are grateful to Bishop Vincent Malone, Episcopal Liaison, for offering his reflection arising from the Joint Dialogue Group (NBCW/ Bishops' Conference), January 2003. We are indebted to the women who gave so readily of their time and energy in the contributions that follow; to Virginia Hearn and the DLT team; and to all those whose thoughts and prayers have helped bring this book to life.

The views expressed in this book are not necessarily the views of the National Board of Catholic Women.

The National Board of Catholic Women

The National Board of Catholic Women actively seeks to promote the presence, participation and responsibilities of Catholic women in the Church and society, in order to enable them to fulfil their evangelical mission and to work for the common good.

With its broad representative base (members of Catholic organisations, national Catholic agencies and bishop-appointed Diocesan Links), the NBCW is a forum for Catholic women which takes their recommendations on the life and mission of the Church to the Bishops' Conference of England and Wales, to which it is a consultative body. It is connected with the universal Church by its representation on the World Union of Catholic Women's Organisations. It forwards to government and others, submissions dealing with matters of concern and public interest. It is actively engaged with many secular, ecumenical and interfaith groups in England and Wales. It is a member of the Women's co-ordinating group of Churches Together in England, the Women's National Commission (a consultative body to the government), the National Council of Women and National Alliance of Women's Organisations. It also has consultative status with the Economic and Social Commission of the United Nations.

NBCW Publications

Do Not Be Afraid – National Consultation of Catholic Women (Redemptorist, 1992)

A Woman's Place: Reflections on Women's Housing Needs (with Catholic Housing Aid Society, 1996)

Raising Awareness of Domestic Violence (1997)

A Guide to the Annulment Process (3rd edition, 1998)

Journey to the Millennium and Beyond – Reflections, Prayers and Poems of Christian Women (1998).

May my husband (a Christian from another faith) receive Holy Communion with me? – How? (pamphlet, 2000)

Breaking the Silence on Domestic Violence (Churches Together in England leaflet, 2001)

The NBCW also produces a quarterly newspaper, *Catholic Omnibus* (formerly *Catholic Woman*). Orders to Andrea Black (Distribution), Gabriel Communications, St James's Building, Oxford Street, Manchester, M1 6FP. Telephone: 0161 236 8856.

Enquiries to The Development Officer, 12 Worsall Road, Yarm, Cleveland, TS15 9DF. Telephone: 01642 791840. Email: enquiries@nbcw.org Website: www.nbcw.org

A MEDITATION

KATE STOGDON

How can the community of the Church engage in true conversation? Perhaps there are some clues in the model of encounter given us in the story of the woman at the well (John 4:1–30).

The well is situated at a crossroads. It is necessary to engage with each other in order to draw the life-giving water from its depths. There is a need to listen, to name, to receive the gift being offered. We come from different directions, have trodden distinctive paths (who is here? – could be here? – is excluded? – has chosen not to be here?).

This is (or could be) a place of encounter. There is a possibility for transformation. Who knows which path will be taken after the conversation. In this meeting, we may find our selves, our hearts broken open and enlarged so that we are changed – converted. We will heal and be healed. We will nourish and be nourished. 'See I am doing a new thing! Do you not perceive it? I am making a way in the desert and streams in the wasteland' (Isa. 43:19). The newness will involve a breaking down, breaking open of the hard heart to reveal the bruised heart of flesh.

The jar in which we have stored our source of nourishment is breaking apart; it can no longer hold the water. The new shape emerging in this dark, quiet, noisy, desperate, hopeful place will be God's shape, enlarging the restricted space in which we have placed this life-giving water, given for all.

Together, can we discover the new container and the new path to travel?

FOREWORD

In 2000, in response to Pope John Paul's call to develop a dialogue with women on 'what it means to be a woman of our time' (Communications Sunday 1996), the National Board of Catholic Women (NBCW) and the Bishops' Conference of England and Wales hosted a conference on that theme. Women and clergy from dioceses across England and Wales met together to explore ways in which the radical transformation of women's lives, especially during the last fifty years, could be seen as a resource for identifying social experience and change as central to an understanding of the Church and its mission in the world.

In 2001, the National Conference of Priests' three-year review of ministry began with the open-ended theme 'Healing Priesthood'; Angela Perkins was invited to contribute an article for their pre-Conference newspaper. Consultations with other women, and further discussion with Verena Wright, suggested strands of thought that went beyond a single article and led to this book project. Clearly, women had many insights to offer from their knowledge and experience of being women 'of our time'. While priests need to be able to reflect together on the present situation and their role in the community, listening to the reflections of lay people – especially women – is vital.

Women involved in specific areas of the Church: media, theology, ministry, education and social justice, were accordingly invited to contribute reflections on healing priesthood from their particular experience, work and vision; these constitute Part 1 of the book. Shorter comment was also sought, principally through *Catholic Woman* (now *Catholic Omnibus*) from 'women in the pews' – the mainstay of parish congregations (Part 2).

Opening to a global perspective, Part 3 contains reflections from contributors actively engaged in the life and mission of the Church throughout the world: connections made possible through the expanding international networks of the NBCW and the speedy communication facilities of the world wide web. What is striking is that many common threads are drawn from the diversity of culture and background in this microcosm of the universal Church.

Since initiating the project, the ordained priesthood has come under increasing scrutiny, nationally and internationally. In some cases the integrity of the Church itself has been called to account. However, this book is not exclusively about the ordained priesthood or women, but about encouraging unity and understanding within the Church.

The world of women has been revolutionised. The world of the priest has changed dramatically. Healing is needed.

The book suggests that perhaps women and clergy share more than is realised. Perhaps together we can make a difference. In sharing insights from faith-based experience and knowledge, women seek to refresh and enable a Church in which the spiritual hunger at the core of our being can be nourished and our common humanity find space and encouragement to grow to fullness.

We hope you will draw insight and inspiration from the challenge of faith and wisdom within these pages.

Angela Perkins
NBCW Development Officer / Editor *Catholic Omnibus*
Verena Wright
Convenor, NBCW Women in the Church Committee
Portsmouth Dioscesan Link

INTRODUCTION

'WHAT IT MEANS TO BE A WOMAN OF OUR TIME' – SPEAKING FROM THE MIDDLE: TOWARDS RENEWED CONVERSATION

ANNA ROWLANDS

The original brief from which these thoughts come was a talk given to the NBCW Joint Dialogue Group Conference in October 2000 about what it means to be women of our time. It began a weekend of dialogue between priests and women from the dioceses of England and Wales. This essay retains from that occasion the serious purpose of proposing that the contemporary experience of women must constitute a significant starting point for a discussion of renewed priesthood.

I offer here a brief sketch of some of the significant factors that lead women into a creative conversation about the role of priesthood in the contemporary world. The stress falls upon the opportunity to begin radically *different* conversations within the Church about the role for a renewed priesthood in dialogue with women. To misuse the work of philosopher Gillian Rose, this middle place of connection that we find ourselves in – between the tradition and our future hope – is a place of deep brokenness, but is our only possible beginning for conversation. I suggest that the enormous changes in women's lives, and the *particular character* of what women *have done* to contribute to the

1

modern world – towards healing brokenness and nourishing those who are broken – and what has been *done to* women – their own brokenness – necessitates a *different* conversation from what has gone before. A familiar theme returns, but quite differently. In identifying some of the issues raised in seeking such a conversation, I suggest that authentic conversation will not be easy and involves a difficult reflection on the contexts from which we speak.

Present Opportunity: Recognising the Positive Challenge

The first challenge for renewed conversation comes from the immense social, economic and political changes that have affected women in the last hundred years. Women are contributing more, in increasingly more varied ways than at any time recognisable within our culture. Equally, the cultural context in which women are living is shaping the possibilities for human thought and being in the world in radically new ways. Within the Church, these broader socio-cultural changes have been experienced intensively in the post-Vatican II period.

Within the socio-economic sphere, the return of many women to the market-place and paid work outside the home has had a profound effect upon the daily reality of their lives; many have gained a degree of financial independence, individually recognised achievements and an existence beyond the domestic family situation. The largest increase in female paid labour has been due to two-thirds of all married women working. Equally significant, 51 per cent of mothers with children under five years old are now in paid work. As Cristina Odone noted on BBC Radio 4's *Thought for the Day* (14 October 2000), 'women are defined by their [paid] work'.[1] Working women now spend more time with colleagues than with their families. This is a seismic change in our daily experience of being women.

Radical developments in genetic, digital and cybernetic technologies demand that we think anew the complex web of connections between gendered humanity and its environment. This opens up old questions and raises new ones about what it is to be 'human' and about the nature of the God who calls us into being. Seemingly abstract, the impact of new technologies is in fact vast, personal and deeply political. Revolutions in health care and domestic technologies, the advent of the cyber world and discourses of 'virtual reality', offer the possibility of a radically changed experience of being a social agent living in a gendered body. Technological change reconfigures the social spaces within which we encounter each other and find our signposts to the divine. We, as Church and as citizens, are called to understand, reflect and contribute to this process of dramatic change.

The promotion and availability of educational opportunities has increased the academic achievements of a wider range of women. Within formal structures, more women are achieving higher qualifications at higher grades than ever before. One can wryly note that the average female PA has more qualifications than her usually male boss. Within our church educational structures, significantly more women are theologically literate, gaining qualifications in a proliferation of courses aimed at the laity. In the Christian churches, women are contributing significantly more in terms of official roles in public worship, the official ritual and sacramental life of the Church, and in renewed structures of pastoral ministry. The quiet revolution that is occurring in patterns of lay ministry in chaplaincy, parish ministry and spirituality and guidance ministry in these isles, is a significant factor in the call for renewed dialogue. For many, it is these women who will come to represent the face of Christian ministry.

Living the Broken Middle: Calling for a Response
However, the complex web within whose living connections women's lives are lived has provided a context of limit and restraint as well as of nurture, support and new opportunity.

The Church's theoretical commitment, made clear during the Synod of Oceania (1998) to 'work to restore the human and Christian dignity of women through the teaching of the Gospel, challenging anything in society or the Church which demeans them', must be made real. Few of the changes affecting women have been unambiguously beneficial or liberating and many contemporary women experience a fragmentary and ambiguous social world in ways hitherto unimagined. For instance, to succeed economically as a woman at present, you are most likely to be a professional, childless and twenty-four years old. Overall, women constitute over 50 per cent of the workforce, concentrated in clerical, secretarial, sales, educational and health work, electronic goods operation and service industries. Women are 70 per cent of the lowest paid and only 10 per cent of the highest paid in Britain today. Women earn on average 60 per cent of what men earn. Per hour women earn on average 79 pence in the male pound; 43% of all female employees earn less than £5 per hour. Over a lifetime, women's earnings will be significantly less than those of men in the same profession: a male nurse will earn £50,000 more than a female nurse due to pay rates, access to overtime and chances of promotion.[2] The vast majority of mothers with children under five do paid work because of financial need. One male wage, where available, is no longer adequate even if it were desired, for most families. Women's opportunities to earn a reasonable wage decline with marriage and children, with caring responsibilities for the elderly as well as the young. This clearly undermines the fabric of family life, the dignity of women and denies the web of connections within which life is sustained.

Poverty, debt and ill health are other significant areas where women experience particular hardship and inequality. However, it is in the international context that women continue to face deep political and economic alienation, physical threat and harm from cultural practices, including suti, female infanticide and cliterodectomy. The shadow of AIDS also brings specific difficulties to women in the developing world. In countries where food is limited, women are much more likely to suffer malnutrition than men, as they feed their families before themselves. In parts of the former Eastern Europe, communities are sustained from the immoral earnings gained by lucrative prostitution. In the Czech Republic, young female students are lured by the promise that they will earn in an hour what their professionally qualified mothers will earn in a month. Every day, third world women are smuggled into European countries to serve as sex slaves, with no papers, no identity and no rights. It is a cruel irony that international NATO personnel stationed in Kosovo, charged with the preservation of vital human rights, have been the impetus behind the smuggling of women to act as forced prostitutes. Even those charged with the special task of protecting human rights do not seem moved by a respect for the dignity of women. It seems easy to concur that 'the so-called free economies are not kind to women who find that they must sell whatever they have that is marketable in order to pay market rates for food and housing.'[3]

Sharing Experience: The Challenges of Conversation

For me, a response to the current moment of opportunity and crisis calls us to silence, to prayer, but also to effective and meaningful dialogue. Communication and encounter with one another begins from our own context, but becomes an ever-widening conversation. In such a spirit Elaine Graham reflects,

> our pastoral practices need to encourage the development of human imagination, embodiment, spirituality, conviviality, all of which may be understood as vital aspects and avenues of personal and collective development. Fundamentally, all these evoke the core metaphor of conversation, an ever wider dialogue between different voices, sources and modes of thinking and being.[4]

However, it is worth stressing that we do come to this dialogue from moments of hope and anguish – and they are related moments. We come also because our tradition offers us a reason to come and a means to explore and articulate such hope and anguish. True knowledge of ourselves, God and each other cannot simply be taught, it can only be gained through experience, encounter with each other and in friendship. Through participation and in collaboration, we can begin to look without blinking into the heart of our brokenness, towards the source of our hope that wells up from this void; but this can only be achieved together, without walking away from that which is difficult and hurtful. This process will also inevitably involve a dialogue with other traditions and systems of thought and being, from which we as a Church have sought to be so separate. Faith is not alien to faith, nor exclusive of reason.

Yet conversation will have its limits too, or rather, its pattern will involve moments of comfortable *and* uncomfortable silence. In a culture where our spaces are filled with public confessional disclosure and permanent background noise, we must not confuse our need for a distinct dialogue with what is just endless chatter – a kind of false immediacy to each other. While we must raise to voice the silenced aspects of women's experience – especially where silence acts as an instrument of oppression – we must also allow an interval for a different silence: one that represents a recognition of difficulty, a space for lament and mourning, and a silence that is simply God's space. In each sense, this silence is paradoxically a sort of listening.

Rosemary Radford Ruether, in dialogue with Thomas Merton, reminds him that collaboration is vital, but that we must not rush into a pseudo-optimism concerning what is possible. This would be the old static triumphalism in a new costume: 'when real contact is made, it is not some immediacy to each other that is best, but authenticity on each of our parts and leaving it to the Holy Spirit to decode the message and help us transform our world'.[5]

Engaging in just such authentic, contextual dialogue must

surely then be one of the tools that will, as Mary McAleese told the Irish National Conference of Priests, allow us to 'tend the garden ... not guard the mausoleum'.[6]

Notes

1. 'Women's Unit Research on Women's Incomes Over a Lifetime (2000)' in *Fawcett Briefing Paper on Equal Pay* 2002.
2. From figures cited in *Fawcett Briefing Paper on Low Pay* 2002. See also www.lowpayunit.org.uk, www.lowpay.gov.uk, www.eoc.org.uk.
3. Germaine Greer, *The Whole Woman* (Doubleday, 1999), p. 7.
4. E. Graham, *Transforming Practices* (Mowbray, 1996), p. 200.
5. 'The Letters of Thomas Merton and Rosemary Radcliffe Ruether' in M. Tardiff (ed.), *At Home in the World* (Orbis, NY), p. 18.
6. Speech given by Mary McAleese to Irish National Conference of Priests, 2000.

PART I

WOMEN'S VOICES
IN ENGLAND
AND WALES

BREAKING OPEN THE WORD OF GOD

ROSEMARY READ

Currently many, perhaps most, priests feel beleaguered: over-worked, undervalued, assumed to be child abusers, blamed for the fact that fewer of us attend church regularly, criticised for being too trendy, too traditional, mediocre or just plain boring. Not a job you would want really, is it? And yet we have so many dedicated, loving, serving priests who need to know they are appreciated.

The words *healing priesthood* bring two thoughts to mind. The first is that priests are healers by nature of their calling; the second that they need healing themselves, more than ever now with the strain and difficulties of the last few years.

Jesus healed in so many ways – restoring sight to the blind, casting out demons, including those who were marginalised by their illness, their sex or their race and he even raised the dead. Priests in the twenty-first century also heal in similar ways – they open our eyes by breaking open the Word of God; they help the distressed (many now as trained counsellors as well as through the sacrament of Reconciliation); they welcome all sorts of out-casts who call at the presbytery or whom they meet in other ways; they anoint the sick and comfort the bereaved. So they heal all sorts of people in all sorts of situations – the best of them most of the time, and all of them some of the time.

But it's a hard job and currently very much under-appreciated. So what can we do?

First of all, I think the laity need to make clear that we don't expect priests to be perfect, or supermen, able to do everything. They are human, and weaknesses should be acknowledged and lay people encouraged to do the things that 'Father' is bad at. Certainly, time for relaxing, reading, praying and in-service training would be more available if priests stopped trying to do those things for which they were not trained. It would also encourage lay people to grow up and to accept the baptismal calling of being 'priest, prophet and king'.

Secondly, I suggest that priests should offer the Eucharistic Liturgy carefully, thoughtfully and not necessarily too often. If the priest consults the people and explains the reasons for Mass time changes and fewer services, we should be adult enough to accept it. Fewer masses, offered and thought about by both lay people and priests might help us all to appreciate and understand it better. I see no evidence in other parts of the world where the celebration of the Eucharist is a rare event, that the Church is dying.

Playing the 'numbers game' is unwise too: it leads to depression, rivalry and often a feeling of failure. Adult Catholics must take responsibility for their actions, whether it is staying away from church, not bringing children to sacramental programmes or not being willing to do anything but put a small amount of money in the plate on Sundays.

It's often a lonely life being a priest – so they need to support each other, whether through praying and reflecting together, eating together or meeting on the golf course. But it is also worth remembering that many of the people priests serve have similar problems. Many people in the parish and local community are lonely too – especially those who have never had the chance to marry and who don't have a high-profile job. They too wonder about their pensions and what will happen to them in their old age. However supportive priests can be of each other, I suggest that discussing such problems in small parish groups where the priest is not expected to be the leader could be helpful and supportive to both priests and people.

But breaking open the Word of God is one of the most important works of the ordained ministry. Of course, this is not exclusively the work of the priest – it is for all the baptised – but the priest does have a leading role, because of the importance of the homily in Sunday and even weekday Eucharists. Sharing the Word is both enriching and healing, however we do it – straightforward homily, shared homily, small discussion groups. It re-creates us, inspires and renews us, to discover anew how to live our faith today. So it should be given that importance in the life and work of the priest. They should be encouraged to go on courses, use biblical commentaries, and reflect with others, both priests and people. I am frequently horrified at the lack of thought put into the homily, which is almost the only occasion most Catholics receive any formation. The amount of effort put into the Word as distinct from the rest of the Eucharistic celebration is in many cases scant in the extreme.

The point is, ultimately priests will not be judged on how many masses they 'said', how many they 'got' into church, how many they 'converted', and certainly not on how many church roofs they stopped leaking. They will be judged, like all of us, on how they proclaimed the Good News to the poor, the lonely and the marginalised – those so often ignored in our church build-ings and our liturgies. I firmly believe that re-emphasising the importance of the Word of God, proclaiming it with renewed enthusiasm and relating it to the world around us would give priests a clearer sense of their role and all of us a clearer focus.

And then maybe people will flock to hear the message of the Good News – that the current mess in our world is not how God wants it to be. Jesus proclaimed a Kingdom amongst us here and now – of peace, justice, love and truth. People are hungry to hear this – priests have a duty to proclaim it and, in doing so, may find clarity and relevance in their ministry.

That would both restore their healing role and be healing for them.

DISCIPLESHIP BEYOND THE BOUNDARIES

ELLEN TEAGUE

I was really cross. There in the distance was Simon, strolling along the country lane and clearly coming to meet me. My nine-year-old son had gone missing from a beach, half a mile away, where I had left him playing nearly two hours earlier. It was more than an hour before my two older sons, cycling around the small Scottish island of Iona, established that he had simply walked back to our holiday accommodation on his own. As I too made my way back, I first occupied my mind with consideration of punishments appropriate for ignoring mother's instructions. Yet, by the time he was close enough for me to make out his smiling face, I was praying for tolerance, resolving both to listen to his explanation and discuss with him ways of avoiding the tensions arising again. Reconciliation is a feature of everyday family life.

The next day the three boys went sea-fishing and, after four hours, had a sizeable catch of pollock and mackerel. But, who would eat it all? Then, a large family moved into our hostel and were happy to accept our offer of sharing the fish. That evening, we all sat down to a truly Eucharistic feast of fresh fish, bread and wine and our separate families became a community of friends for the days we had left together.

My understanding of sacrament goes beyond the boundaries of church and family. For me, Reconciliation embraces structural injustice and the degradation of God's creation as well as individual sin; Eucharist, too often perceived as a ritual with little relevance outside Sunday Mass observance, cries out for action to bring about a just sharing of the world's food resources between rich and poor; Baptism, with its use of water to symbolise new life, draws me to campaign for clean water for poor Third World communities. This broad awareness of sacrament is demonstrated in some of the Church's teaching. In 2000, Catholic bishops of North-west USA and Canada released a Pastoral Letter calling for a new environmental and spiritual awareness about the polluted Columbia River, the region's main waterway. The bishops called the river a 'sacramental commons', where people can experience the Creator in creation, outside formal church settings.

There are clearly implications here for a sacramental ordained priesthood that, despite modern ecumenical, interfaith and secular engagement, remains ritualistic, elite and male. Yet the Vatican seems not to welcome dialogue, and vigorously protects the anachronism of a centralised leadership style that is more about clerical empire than Christian community. Discussion about whether married priests might administer sacraments in dioceses facing clergy shortages is not welcomed. Liberal priests and bishops are not affirmed by the institution. Women with priestly vocations – and their supporters who question total sacramental dependence on men – are simply ignored. Women's creative perspectives on such things as liturgy, design of worship spaces, pastoral ministry and formation impinge quietly, but remain unrecognised. Is it any wonder that non-ordained Catholics, male or female, rarely see themselves as active participants in the Church's mission to bring good news to the poor and to heal?

The marginalisation of women has prevented the Church from developing its notion of priesthood. The Indian journalist Dr Astrid Lobo Gajiwala, reflecting on women's ministry, tells the story of waiting in the parlour of an archbishop's house with her friend, Nivedita, who spied stone images of previous cardinals engraved on the walls: "'Who are they?" she wanted to know. "Big priests," I answered. "But why their photo is up there?" she persisted. "Because they were good," I said, giving them the benefit of the doubt. "They are kind; they loves children?" she innocently asked. Did they? I silently wondered.'[1] According to Dr Gajiwala, the lack of closeness to children diminishes a priest's ministry, and indeed the Church. I too have often felt that women's close experience of birthing and raising the young sensitises them to suffering and prompts practical responses. I remember crying over TV pictures of starving people in Ethiopia as I breast-fed my first child. At last I truly understood the frantic sucking of a child on a dry breast and the despair of the mother. It is not surprising that CAFOD, and a number of church initiatives which tackle injustice, were originally founded by women's groups in the Church.

Women's ministry is a non-ritualised service from one human being to another in the name of Christ. A 1994 US study high-lighted that 85 per cent of non-ordained ministerial positions in parishes were held by women.[2] Based on my own observations, I suspect a similar figure would apply in Britain. Women tend towards an affective rather than an intellectual approach to the knowledge of God. Dr Gajiwala calls for a priesthood infused with the wisdom of women's ministry in

> 'their capacity for relationship, that bonds not just person to person, but the human to the earth and God within us; their spirituality, that recognises no boundaries between the sacred and life, but instead leads them to live every ordinary, heartbreaking, exquisite, inspiring moment in relation to God; their ability to remain connected through systems that encourage *power-with* and *power-among* and *power-for*, rather than *power-over*; and their closeness to life, that makes them so vulnerable to love that they cannot help but be moved to serve.'

She calls this '*the ministry of the Gospels*'.[3]

So, what form could *healing priesthood* take? It would move towards more genuine partnership between ordained priest-hood and the *priesthood of all believers*, whose role in the Church's mission was affirmed by the Second Vatican Council. There would be less emphasis on institution, patriarchy and rules; more on building community, lay formation, lay membership of parish teams, and justice and peace outreach. Openness to a gradual transformative process would mean encouraging dialogue where questions about the nature and meaning of priesthood can be heard, rather than blocked. Women theologians such as Rosemary Radford Ruether and Joan Chittister offer fascinating insights. They suggest that true discipleship is not membership of a clerical club called 'Church', but a mission, alongside other people of God, to bring healing to a world plagued by injustice, violence, and depletion of the earth's resource base.[4]

Notes

1. *The Month*, May 1997. Dr Gajiwala is head of the Tissue Bank, Tata Hospital, Mumbai and received Best Christian Journalist of India Award 1996.
2. Quoted in *Strengthening the Bonds of Peace: a Pastoral Reflection on Women in the Church and in Society*, Conference of Catholic Bishops 1994.
3. *ibid.*
4. See e.g. Joan Chittister, *Heart of Flesh: A Feminist Spirituality for Women and Men* (William B. Eerdmans, 1998); Rosemary Radford Ruether, *Women Healing Earth* (SCM Press, 1996).

'PERFECT LOVE DRIVES OUT FEAR'

SR LOUISE SWANSTON SSMN

The priesthood is a healing vocation. And yet, 'Physician, heal yourself' (Luke 4:23) seems horribly apposite today.

I have no problem with the concept of a healing priesthood, as I know priests who habitually seek out the lost and bandage the wounded. Most of my priestly colleagues have been gentle and pastoral, unassuming, humble and hard-working; compassionate towards their 'flock', if not uniformly towards me. The parish Sister can be a convenient punch-bag on 'bad hair days'!

Some years ago, I worked as a school chaplain in collaboration with eleven visiting priest-chaplains. They co-operated well and did all in their power to bring the Good News to a bunch of giddy, often 'religiously-challenged' teenagers. Whether these priests were progressive (few were!) or arch-traditionalist (some were), the prime focus was the welfare of those in their care. However, I did run into trouble at one end-of-year Mass when six teenage girls choreographed a dance for the offertory procession, based on St Ignatius' 'Take, Lord, receive . . .'. Although eight of the eleven celebrants seemed happy with the draft I sent out, three bristled at the word 'dance' on the programme. They said so in letters of complaint. Two were impolite; the third expressed sadness that the liturgy should be so dishonourably celebrated. He was a most lovable man, and a wounded healer in every respect, but I could not justify altering the liturgy at the eleventh hour. Sadly, those priests were applying their vivid imaginations, sight unseen, and turning the dance into a demon. They little knew what time, energy and sheer love those girls invested. The dance itself, reverent and deeply moving, went forward in spite of, and without, the three conscientious objectors.

Agonising over such conflict seems futile. Probably control, male–female issues, arch-conservatism and lack of imagination all played their part, but I doubt if malice featured. Certainly, the contretemps was anything but healing.

Years later, I worked in a parish. The parish priest championed laity, religious, women, children, the disabled and refugees, recognising and encouraging individual gifts, giving people a sense of worth and dignity. The African priest who assisted him had a unique gift in the confessional, which meant healing ministry was strong in that parish. It remains so today under new leadership.

I have met various confessors and retreat-givers who effectively mediate Christ's healing. One heard my confession non-judgementally after a gap of fifteen years; another even asked me to place my hands on his head and say the prayers of absolution with him. I appreciate the sensitivity and courage these men display! 'Perfect love drives out fear' (1 John 4:18); but then the reverse is also true.

Working on mixed teams (priests, religious and laity), one senses that *perfect fear* of doing the wrong thing blocks many priests from doing even what would be acceptable, e.g. finding suitable preaching opportunities for the non-ordained, or taking advantage of Canon Law Rule 230 paragraph 3, which allows laity to baptise in extremis. I have always found deanery meetings a trial: women think differently from priests, having less to lose for being adventurous, and soon begin to feel sidelined. Recently, however, I worked on the Executive Committee of the Conference of Religious; there I encountered greater parity, chiefly because the Conference is collaborative and there are far more women than men.

Priestly healers vastly outnumber priestly abusers. To augment their healing ministry, we need to liberate priests to heal. To that end, two priorities suggest themselves: firstly, to prise priests out from behind their desks so they can address their people's pastoral needs; secondly, to make monthly attendance at a clerical support group mandatory for every priest. Some do this already. Our task-orientated Church generates too many working parties and ongoing planning projects. These drive priests away from the human and spiritual needs of fellow-priests and parishioners alike and prevent them from taking care of themselves.

I am not an expert on seminary training. I only know that most priests trained in the last fifteen years appear even more ill at ease with their sexuality than their predecessors. Insofar as this suggests lack of psycho-spiritual integration input at the seminary, then I recommend its immediate injection. The brokenness needs healing. Statistics have long suggested a high percentage of homosexuals in Britain's seminaries. This, if true, is a neutral fact, for the Church has nothing against the orientation itself. Therefore, perhaps it is unnecessary and unhelpful to purvey such information, applying labels and creating a climate of divisiveness. Young men full of zeal for the Lord's work are feeling over-scrutinised, and for the wrong reasons. When they leave in disillusionment, the Church is robbed of their healing ministry.

Younger priests also seem strangely uncomfortable with the subjects of prayer and vocations. Does that indicate further lacunae in seminary training? To experience Christ's healing love, we need help with prayer. If priests are uneasy with it, perhaps they should call on parishioners. Many women seem to have a special gift for this. As for vocations, *Pastores Dabo Vobis* (para. 41) is clear that 'all the members of the Church have the grace and responsibility to look after vocations';[1] traditionally, vocations come from families, but how many feel confident enough to encourage them?

In conclusion, many people still attribute their experience of God to the influence of healing pastors. Conversely, I have seen relatives and friends slowly lose faith, not in God, but in the institutional Church. I have also seen the light die in the eyes of dearly loved priests, who give up through disillusionment, burnout or a call to marriage. I have sometimes seen the Church fail in its healing ministry to these men.

I have witnessed priests working indefatigably, despite being hurt and rejected. I know the fear of some priests, whose pastoral theology gives them more compassion than the institutional Church would allow them to express. It is sad that such good men have to mistrust their own shadows – knowing they would be written off as mavericks if Church authorities knew how compassionate they dared to be. All this works against the healing power of the priesthood.

Official cover-ups will no longer protect us from scandal: we need to acknowledge the borderline between respectful discretion and secrecy. And what makes dioceses assume that offering vast sums to victims of clerical abuse will 'buy back' their psychosexual health? Or that we can justify stifling other aspects of the Church's life as we cream off all the funds? Or that church members can continue to insult homosexually-orientated priests by assuming they are practising, or by simplistically associating homosexuality with paedophilia? Or wound those genuinely called to celibacy by suggesting married priests would solve the child-abuse issue?

The Church's future is probably in the hands of the laity. But as priest numbers continue to decline, we might ask the question which only time will answer: is this diminishment a haemorrhage or a purification? Is the priesthood undergoing slow death or slow healing?

Note
1. Post-Synodal Apostolic Exhortation of Pope John Paul II, March 1992.

'SO WE CALL EVERYONE PRIESTS ...'[1]

PAT JONES

It does not surprise me that priesthood is experiencing times of crisis in the present context in which the Church finds itself: a culture and society confused about meaning, profoundly influenced by the media and largely caught up in an ethic of consumerism. Some of the profound tensions between the gospel and our present lives, between the Church as a community seeking a radical fidelity to Christ, and a world bewilderingly full of both goodness and suffering, seem inevitably to be visible in the experience of ordained priesthood. It does not surprise me either that, despite all this, among those who are ordained priests there is found holiness, great depths of service to people, immense solidarity with the poor, courage and conviction.

I find it hard to propose what will 'heal' priesthood. I recognise that some individuals may need 'healing', and that perceptions of priesthood have been damaged in recent years, but I am also conscious that, doctrinally and in practice, ordained priesthood is evolving and developing. It's not static and I doubt that the reality is ever finished or perfect. I suspect that all of us, priests or baptised lay people, are always in need of healing; indeed, the whole Church, as Vatican II reminded us, is always in need of renewal. The present times may indeed feel more threatening for some, and priesthood more endangered but, for others, the present challenges may be opening up space for the gospel and for the priesthood in ways that were not possible before. In this context, perhaps I can express a couple of hopes and convictions about what may be important for priesthood to flourish.

After some twenty years working within the Church at various levels, my deepest conviction about priesthood is about the mutuality that exists between the priesthood of the baptised and ordained ministry. John O'Donoghue, the Irish poet and priest, expresses it thus: ordained priesthood exists 'to awaken and realize the implicit priestliness of each person ... priesthood is ministry to the deepest nature and identity of the person. It attempts to bring the hidden rhythm of our priestliness to awareness and realization'.[2] This is a profound vision of how an aspect of each person's humanity can be brought to life, in and through the smallest of interactions and the details of daily living, as well as through larger choices and actions. It points to the quality of relationships between priests and people as a primary place of ministry, whatever the focus of each interaction. Admittedly it makes priesthood more demanding; no concealing of one's humanity in a role or functions will achieve the authentic and personal impact that awakens the priestliness of others, whether or not it is named as such.

The priestliness of lay baptised people is active first of all in the activities and relationships that make up daily life. It is expressed in compassion, in comforting and forgiving, in gathering people, in treating people or precious things reverently, in the costly self-giving of being a parent or a community activist, and in many other ways. It is this priestliness that ordained priests can evoke, affirm or strengthen. So I see hope for the future of priesthood in paying a new kind of attention to the patterns of relationship and collaboration between priests and laity. The previous culture of seeing priests as 'set apart' or in some way superior needs to give way to a different kind of mutual pastoral relationship. This has already been growing for some time, but the growth is uneven and probably underfed, not least because the issues that attract attention and energy are often institutional.

One powerful example that I see before me in a different way since working at CAFOD is about compassion. In CAFOD's *Reflections for Advent 2002*, 'God is With Us', Donal O'Leary comments at one point that 'we are genetically coded for compassion'. It's a strength of Christian faith community to keep this precious capacity alive and rooted in something deeper than guilt or easy emotionalism. The Catholic community has immense compassion, as CAFOD knows well from the generous response given to appeals and fast days. We know very well too how much difference it makes when these invitations to compassion and solidarity are supported and deepened by what priests can say and do to link them to faith and mission. It is a kind of priestliness to express compassion, whether it is immediate or global. It is a valuable sacramental role when ordained priests symbolise and name that capacity and call to compassion.

Some of these newer patterns of relationship between priests and people bring this priestliness to life within ecclesial community, through ministries and other kinds of shared leadership and collaboration. Many priests and bishops, along with many lay people, are already deeply convinced that this is where the future of the Church lies. Yet we don't have many structures or strategies or serious allocation of resources that recognise it and show our commitment to take it seriously. It still feels as though collaborative ministry is an optional side interest rather than a mainstream direction; this limits confidence and growth. One of my hopes would be for significant and visible commitments to this pastoral model.

I see the present times for priesthood not as times of crisis, but rather as opportunities for new and courageous commitments and models. We still need the distinctive presence and ministry of ordained priests among us, but the context is different and the challenges to Catholic faith are immense. We need priests who are excited and hopeful in the face of these challenges, who engage with the cultural, political and social realities around us, and work with us to discern how to be and how to act.

Notes

1. St Augustine.
2. John O'Donoghue, 'The Priestliness of the Human Heart' in *The Way Supplement* (1995–8).

TO LOVE IS TO BE VULNERABLE

PIA BUXTON IBVM

I believe that grace and growth most abound when people slow down and reflect, face their pain and darkness, and dare to speak of it in truth ... It is this honesty that is healing and liberating, hence the reflective exercises suggested here.

To be healed requires acknowledging our woundedness and the courage to share it; this truth makes us vulnerable and human, liberates us from the weight of deception, and frees us for healing others. This is the universal task, within the gospel calling, of the priestly heart. It applies to the ordained and the non-ordained, to the institutional Church as a whole and at all levels. It abounds in grace.

We constantly hear that the Church is in crisis. The word 'crisis' is depicted by two characters in Chinese: the character for opportunity and the character for danger. The danger is to build fortifications; the opportunity is to risk being vulnerable.

Real faith, and the freedom it brings, are experienced when we risk not giving priority to self-preservation.

Exercise 1: Ponder these words concerning faith and not giving priority to self-preservation in regard to (i) your own life; (ii) the life of your parish/ministry; (iii) the life of the institutional Church; (iv) examples from the Gospel which come to mind.

Today, many in the Church, particularly its ordained members, are bewildered and often in pain. For some there is a faith crisis, perhaps an overwhelming spiritual darkness. Such experience is evident at diverse times in the Church's history and also, inevitably, in the faith journey of the individual who seeks God seriously and tries to follow Jesus. In the fourteenth century Meister Eckhart wrote:

> What is this darkness? What is its name?
> Call it: an aptitude for prayer.
> Call it: a rich sensitivity which will make you whole.
> Call it: an aptitude for vulnerability.

Exercise 2: (i) Face and name significant darkness in your own inner life and go and share it with a friend or, even better, a group of friends; (ii) bear in mind that 70 per cent of our treasure lies in our wounds; (iii) spend a little while with the fragility of Jesus in Gethsemane.

Our work of healing and of being healed expresses the continuing mission of the Word incarnate, the empathy of God revealed among us. The word 'empathy' has the same root as 'passion'; it goes further than 'sympathy' or 'compassion'. It means walking in the shoes of another. The t'ai chi expression of this generosity and desire for union is an extending of the arms in a gesture that is more passive than active, a vulnerable defenceless position, resembling the physical shape of the crucified – the kenosis, the self-emptying of Jesus.

To Pilate's question, 'What is truth?' Jesus gave no spoken answer, just the lived expression of the truth that to love, in the human context, is to be vulnerable.

Perhaps that is what we are all waiting for – a model of Church imitating the self-emptying, the kenosis of Christ: 'the empty Church'. The institutional Church, with its male celibate clerics and consequent susceptibility to power and secrecy, is always called to follow Jesus, to live in union with the living Christ and therefore to give absolute priority to the liberation and vitality of truth. We sometimes see the power of this kenosis in individuals. They shine with hope and inspire with wonder; we see Christ in these wounded healers.

> The other Gods were strong,
> But Thou wast weak.
> They strode,
> But Thou went stumbling to the throne.
> Yet only God's wounds
> To our wounds can speak,
> And no other God has wounds
> Save Thou alone.

Exercise 3: (i) *Reflect on this model of Church. How does it relate to healing priesthood? (ii) Reflect on the words: As has often been realised but not always witnessed to, the Gospel cannot be preached from a position of power. What small steps, perhaps quite practical ones, need to be taken in your parish/ministry to express powerlessness?*

So what is the role of women in this? Since ours is a non-ordained priesthood, we cannot participate in the feminine sacramental expressions of life-giving and feeding, let alone healing and absolving, and most of us probably do not want to. But something is happening at the base line of the pyramid – among the roots and first signs of life, where women are. Down there is an awakening to the Spirit that blows where it will and heals wherever the heart is open to healing. This awakening is fostered by friendship and listening, by waiting and conversation. It is happening across the churches – even crossing faith-boundaries. Like the music of the Kingdom, you have to listen carefully for it and be open to surprises.

Among Christians today there is obvious apathy about official religion, the sacramental life and church teaching. Yet spirituality abounds; there is a genuine seeking of truth and a commitment to prayer among many, of all types and ages. The feminine in us all, men and women, has a particular capacity for intuitive listening, for sensing pain and for walking beside those who are wounded or hungry. This healing experience happens at a deeper level than the external signs of formal sacrament; it can happen anywhere, among strangers or close friends, in pairs or small groups, in conversation or silent listening. It is not an exclusive, universal, timeless human ministry of healing.

Women do much of this work: spiritual listening and sharing, prayer guidance and accompanying. It is an intuitive gift, requiring a genuine and tested aptitude and training, but those doing it are seldom part of any authority structure or hier-archical position. It is seldom appreciated or recommended by clergy and not much used by them, yet it could play a significant part in *healing priesthood*, whether for ordained priests or, with support from the Church, an accredited and appreciated parish ministry.

Women have often been branded 'gossips'. The word origi-nally described the support of one woman for another in childbirth: an 'ordinary' life-giving healing ministry, where an encouraging friend listened, gossiped and cheered a mother through her pain as she brought forth new life. Perhaps that is another emerging model: The Gossiping Church.

Exercise 4: *(i) Reflect on the current role and potential of the feminine in healing priesthood; (ii) what new meaning might the model of 'The Gossiping Church' bring to healing and life-giving in your parish or ministry?*

Note
1. Edward Shillito, *Jesus of the Scars* (1918), cited in J. Stott, *The Cross of Christ* (Intervarsity Press, 1989).

'YOU ARE AN IKON – A GLIMPSE OF THE UNSEEN GOD … LET ME DRINK IN YOUR HEALING PRESENCE'[1]

ANGELA HARPHAM

A healing ministry is one where people flourish; it has open doors, a breath of fresh air. It is engaged with people, enabling them to walk side by side as adults. In order to include women I use the words healing ministry, rather than healing priesthood.

Cultivating a healing presence is a bit like cultivating a garden, because it requires time and attention, some knowledge of the conditions, and what will grow there. There are specific skills of healing, essential ways of being with people – an ability to sit with pain, my own and others', to speak of unspeakable things, to listen deeply and notice what is going on in me, and those I am with. To be attentive and provide a secure base for fears and rage to be spilled out and where tears flow to aid inner healing. Drawing threads between immediate distress and how religious or spiritual life promotes healing or causes suffering. Helping some folk to be well again and to recover shattered hopes, and lost dreams.

When people are psychologically unwell and their belief systems are shattered they require time and the presence of someone to sit, honour the pain and quietly listen at depth in the confusion. But it is also important to look through the messiness for sunbeams, to help discover the starlight and share knowledge, to believe in them. Healing comes unseen.

My origins are not within the Catholic Church. My birth family thought religion was dubious; there was school religion and I had my 'private' god whom I talked to when I was lonely or frightened. Throughout my childhood, the seeds of faith came in different guises. I sometimes went to Sunday School at the Primitive Methodist Church with a friend, where I loved the hymn singing. She played the piano and I sang at school assemblies. On summer evenings near our new house I joined others to listen to the Salvation Army, who collected money from those who went to the greyhound races. They played instruments and encouraged us to sing hymns. I was a fervent little girl who sang from her heart 'Jesus wants me for a sunbeam'. The Salvation Army helped those in need; their ministry was joyful and rooted in action.

Another important influence on me was my last teacher. She believed in us and called forth things from me that bear fruit now. She taught us to 'bear ourselves with dignity' and, more importantly for me because I had failed the 11-plus, shared intellectual knowledge. I learned that she was a Christian, but not from her lips; she left a lingering something, the presence of spiritual communion.

Three ideas caught from these childhood experiences – 'Jesus wants me for a sunbeam', 'Actions speak louder than words', 'Knowledge is power'– have been the underground springs that have fed my life and continue to underpin my ministry.

Jesus said, 'I am come that you may have life, life in abundance'. People then and now have had profound effects on me and some will never know the abundance they gave to me; they were and are part of a healing ministry which Anne Herbert describes as 'random kindness and senseless acts of beauty'.[2] Their loving abundant extravagance helped me to hang on to my dreams and continue my restless longing. My image of healing ministry is a resounding YES to the cosmos at the annunciation.

A year after marriage I became a Roman Catholic, to fulfil a dormant and deep longing to express openly a faith I had quietly kept since childhood. Being married and raising three sons to adulthood was a big part of my training for ministry, as is the volunteer work I have done as a counsellor for marriage and relationships, and for those less fortunate. For almost thirty-four years I have asked questions I now realise I was not supposed to ask. It hit me with a piercing clarity that when I said yes to Roman Catholicism, as a woman I gave away my baptismal birthright to seal that childhood call – vocation to priesthood. The lack of priests in our diocese opened up an opportunity for me to minister as health care chaplain and in part answer that call.

Once in ministry I experienced tension between the traditional sacramental clerical priesthood and the commissioned ministry of lay people. For some priests, the emphasis seems to be on 'me' the priest, 'my' celibacy, and who is worthy to receive 'my' ministry rather than on extravagant giving to others. I was shocked to discover that, for some, I did not know my place as a lay woman. I have become aware of misogyny from Roman Catholic men and women. I have felt restricted and limited in my potential ministry because of the teaching authority of the Roman Catholic Church. I endure the pain of being silenced from even discussing the possibility of ordained ministry for women.

In contrast to some of these negative experiences, ministry in health care chaplaincy with Roman Catholic lay women colleagues has provided me with a deep sense of mission, encouragement, honesty and fun. My Anglican colleagues enriched my theology, and my nurse supervisor and the occupational therapists' trust and belief in me has been heart-warming in some challenging times.

The phrase 'physician heal thyself' in ministry poses questions. What of those who remain troubled? Who needs to be healed? Whose needs are we ministering to? Who is the healer? Where is the healing for those who feel rejected on grounds of gender from full participation in the healing ministry?

Nevertheless, whilst lay people are unable to break bread,

administer the sacrament of Reconciliation and anoint with healing oils those in psychological or physical pain, their healing ministry is alive and active – speaks out against injustice, uncovers sunbeams, shares knowledge, discovers starlight.

Notes

1. Angela Harpham, unpublished poem.
2. Anne Herbert et al., *Random Kindness and Senseless Acts of Beauty* (Volcano Press, 1993).

FIRE, FAITH AND
FRIENDSHIP

SR MARY PIA ODC

'Go to my brethren and tell them that I am ascending to my
Father and your Father, to my God and your God.'[1] These are
almost the first words of the risen Christ: his proclamation of
the Good News of the resurrection, yes; but also the opening of
a window into the mystery of God's new creation. Surely he is
inviting us into his own filial relationship with his Father, that we
may become a 'people made one with the unity of the Father,
the Son and the Holy Spirit.'[2] By sending Mary Magdalen as
his messenger to the apostles, Jesus announces that all his followers are one family, that status is not for them, but rather
friendship. At the Last Supper, he had specifically warned that,
'it must not be so among you' since 'I am among you as one who
serves',[3] and, 'I call you friends'.[4] A new relationship with God
can only issue in a new relationship among ourselves.

How do we grasp the height, depth, breadth of such Good
News? Every generation is called afresh to this supreme mystery.
It was the bedrock of Vatican II. 'By her relationship with Christ,
the Church is a kind of sacrament of intimate union with God,
and of the unity of all mankind'[5] – a clarion-call for our times.
Yet, here we seem to be, bogged down in destructive crisis.

As a Teresian Carmelite, I belong to a tradition which has
always seen prayer for God's priests as an important part of our
vocation. Our community has no fixed chaplain, but is served
by a number of excellent priests. This is a real gift of God, and
an antidote to any doubts about the genuine holiness and good-

ness of many contemporary priests. However, it happens that several priests – young, middle-aged and even elderly – have shared with me some deeply distressing 'shadow' aspects of the priesthood as it is lived out by some. I've heard some real horror stories. But what comes across as the most crushing and widespread problem is less dramatic. Simply, many priests are perceived (by fellow priests as well as laity) as having lost the vision of their vocation. The fire has gone. Let me repeat, we in our community are in touch with many truly inspiring priests, so this is definitely not a universal malaise. But it does seem far-reaching.

Truly, *healing priesthood* is double-edged. The priesthood exists for the healing of God's people, and, at the same time, it (like the Church herself) is always in need of healing. Yes, always, not just nowadays. We are all sinners, and shall always be in need of healing. The ultimate source can only be God: Christ's Spirit poured out through sacraments and scriptures; through prayer and Christian community; in a special way through the Eucharist. But each one of us is called to be a healing minister for others. Isn't it part of the incarnation that Jesus is not only Word-made-flesh, but also chooses to come to us in each other?

So what am I saying? Firstly, I'm hoping for a deep spiritual renewal among our brothers in the priesthood, and especially in the way that prospective priests are trained. I'm hoping that personal prayer, the Word of God, and a 'vital and vitalising'[6] celebration of the Eucharist and other sacraments (especially Reconciliation) will increasingly become a driving force in their lives. For us – God's people – our priests are an irreplaceable channel of grace. And while immediate preparation is vital for good celebration, it is ultimately the quality of personal friendship with Christ that 'speaks'. Secondly, I believe there is a tremendous need for greater trust and friendship throughout God's people. Priests, like others, need to be loved and supported, perhaps now more than ever, when they are suffering such painful and humiliating suspicion.

I've come across suggestions that seminaries should return to the practice of older devotions. I think the Spirit may be calling in a different direction today. There is a real hunger for faith-sharing, especially among the young, above all faith-sharing based on the Word of God (ideally in harmony with the current liturgical readings). I would like this prioritised in seminary formation, and also in parishes. Not only does it nourish our love of God and vitalise our liturgy, it also nourishes deep inter-personal relationships, allowing God's Spirit to work through each one for the good of all.

Another contemporary hunger is for contemplative prayer, with a maturing recognition that it is open to all the baptised. This is not new. The old farmer who told the Curé of Ars: 'I just looks at 'im and 'e looks at me' – well, that's classic! St Teresa too had sensible views: in touch with many 'contemplative' lay people as well as diocesan clergy, she saw prayer as 'a friendly conversation with one who we know loves us'.[7] She was also convinced that love is the great healer for all wounds. Do we not all – laypeople, priests and religious alike – need to 'draw near with confidence to the throne of grace',[8] the heart of Jesus, wounded for love of us, the wellspring of love, wholeness and healing?

I believe there is also a need to face and heal the man/woman relationship. It would be simplistic to imagine that this is ever 'easy'. But it is always deeply rewarding, and surely a vital part of integrated Christian maturity. (How beautifully Jesus related to women in the Gospels!) I'm told that many priests are afraid of women; on the other hand, there are a good many women (especially, perhaps, apostolic women religious) who feel tremendous anger with the clergy. Neither of these attitudes will lead to growth. Genesis pictures us as needing each other (and then going on to blame each other!). I'm told that at the 1994 Roman Synod on Religious Life, the Pope actually said, informally, that the mystery of God is so great that it needs to be explored by men and women together. Obviously he wasn't referring to the ordination of women. Probably he was talking about theology, but it applies equally to spirituality – *and* to the day-to-day living out of the Christian life. In our diocese, it is suggested that women take part in deanery meetings (it already happens in a few), and the whole area of collaborative ministry is a primary growing-point. We need to explore ways of becoming more truly 'Christian family' at every level. Let us explore together! Friendship is born and grows when we share our projects, hopes, dreams, and work together to face the pain and adventures involved. There is so much pain about. We need each other's compassion and friendship, rooted in the compassion and friendship of Christ.

Notes

1. John 20:17.
2. St Cyprian, quoted in *Lumen Gentium* No. 4.
3. Luke 22:26–7.
4. John 15:14.
5. *Lumen Gentium* No. 1.
6. *Presbyterorum Ordinis* No. 5.
7. St Teresa of Avila, *Life, viii.*
8. Hebrews 4:16.

WHERE ANGELS FEAR
TO TREAD

KATHRYN TURNER

It is 19.35 on Wednesday 20 November, 2002. Not a time or date that may mean much as you read this but, at the time of writing, Myra Hindley's funeral is taking place. Not a Requiem Mass, but a short crematorium service as – in the perhaps unfortunate words of Jonathan Miller on that evening's BBC *Front Row* radio programme, 'even this appalling woman is being accorded a funeral of some sort' – her final rite of passage into – whatever lies beyond.

The minister was a Roman Catholic priest – had it been another minister, would that attitude have been tenable or gone quite so unchallenged?

As a Church, we are called to face many challenges, but this is perhaps one of the greatest: how do we receive so obvious a sinner as a sister, a member of the Body of Christ? Is it possible? Is it desirable? And if so, how can that be brought about?

Our biggest problem lies in our founder. If only he had set a good example – mixing with the great and the good and saying the right things at the right time. Instead, we get a man who was noticeably unconcerned about public opinion – darnit! He was not a media man: he just was – and is – himself.

And yet, in a way that is almost impossible to fathom, he used the media of the day to spread his message. He did not have access to radio and television – let alone the Internet – and the mysteries of producing a press release would undoubtedly have raised a wry smile! His message was conveyed in what he was, in what he did, and in what he commissioned his disciples to do: to go and heal, cast out spirits, raise the dead.

It is a message that applies to everyone, and the ways in which we do it may extend the meaning to healing emotional pain, to casting out the materialistic spirits of the age, and to raising those who, in the eyes of society, and maybe their own, are dead – irrelevant – of no use.

It is a message that applies to everyone, but some are asked to take it a step further, to stand as witnesses by devoting a lifetime – with all its joys and sorrows – to that mission. Some are called to stand out from the crowd – to take the risk of being seen as a Catholic priest.

At a time when revelations of child abuse by clergy are unfolding, what courage must it take for a man to say that he is a Catholic priest. What trust can be placed in him by victim and perpetrator alike when, under the seal of confession, they place into his hands things that could not be placed anywhere else. He will not record the interview. He will not report to a committee. He will receive in the love of Christ the pain and, one prays, the remorse and, by the grace of God, take both along the path of healing.

As people responded to the immediate anguish of September 11, was it entirely accidental that the first recorded death was that of a Catholic priest ministering to one of God's people? How often had he administered the sacrament? How often do *our* priests administer the sacrament? And yet, in the glare of publicity, suddenly the world was made aware of its power – to heal when hope was gone, to heal when hope only survived in the promise of eternal life. An ordinary priest going about an extraordinary work spoke to a shattered world of the powerful healing love of God. A healing love that endures beyond death.

And so we come to a crematorium, and a woman who committed grave sin, and a Catholic priest conducting her funeral. What could he say? Nothing that would satisfy those who do not believe in redemption, remorse, forgiveness. But he could speak of his Master, on whom he has modelled, however imperfectly, his life. One who dined with sinners – to the consternation of the 'great and good' – who touched the unclean and made them whole. One who raised those who had died to a second chance for living. One who forgave sin first – and asked questions later.

So we come back to a man – a Catholic priest at the foot of the coffin of one of the most notorious women of the twentieth century. The media did not show itself in its best light: a pack of people preying on the worst. And in the midst of it all, a few people, led by a priest, praying for the best – for the healing of a very damaged soul touched by evil, and the healing of those kept in agony by memories gleefully resurrected by a secular press.

We believe in resurrection – that our Lord died and was raised to new life. Priests and people alike are called to bear witness to that truth.

But it is our priests perhaps who identify themselves most evidently with the message. Death gives way to life, sin gives way to redemption, the people of God are fed, and the Master's work is done.

The funeral of a despised woman; the bedside of someone dying a lingering death; the home of people with no money on which to live; the cell of the unwelcome stranger to our country; the confessional in which, at last, someone lays down the burden of years ... These are all lonely places into which angels – let alone the secular press – would fear to tread. It is the place to which the Master calls everyone – clergy and lay ...

But few are called to witness to the existence of this place so publicly – to declare that, in the face of evil and pain, Christ's ministry to his people is, at its simplest and starkest, to be in the darkest of places – to witness to the light of an enduring and healing love.

WOUNDED HEALERS:
THE HEALING MINISTRY OF
PRIESTS AND WOMEN

TINA BEATTIE

Henri Nouwen, in his book *The Wounded Healer*, says of the minister, 'Whether he tries to enter into a dislocated world, relate to a convulsive generation, or speak to a dying man, his service will not be perceived as authentic unless it comes from a heart wounded by the suffering about which he speaks.'[1] Nouwen quotes a legend from the Jewish Talmud, which tells of the people who are waiting for a Messiah to liberate them from their sufferings:

> Rabbi Yoshua ben Levi came upon Elijah the prophet while he was standing at the entrance of Rabbi Simeron ben Yohai's cave ... He asked Elijah, 'When will the Messiah come?' Elijah replied,
> 'Go and ask him yourself.'
> 'Where is he?'
> 'Sitting at the gates of the city.'
> 'How shall I know him?'
> 'He is sitting among the poor covered with wounds. The others unbind all their wounds at the same time and then bind them up again. But he unbinds one at a time and binds it up again, saying to himself, "Perhaps I shall be needed: if so I must always be ready so as not to delay for a moment."'[2]

Nouwen's short book is a profound meditation on ministry,

suffering and healing which was first published in 1979, but it is interesting to note how much has changed since then. He focuses almost exclusively on relationships between and amongst men, and the book says nothing about the deep but hidden wounds that have been inflicted on the body of the Christian Church in the area of gender and sexuality. Today, these issues have become an open wound in the body of the Church, so that it is not possible to speak about the healing ministry without speaking about healing our understanding of what it means to relate to one another as sexual beings, as male and female made in the image of God.

Women and priests in the modern Catholic Church have much in common. Together, we are counting the cost of a history of repression and denial. In the inability to celebrate God's great gift of sexuality, the Church has inflicted many psychological and physical wounds because of a pessimistic theology which is too preoccupied by the dangers of sexuality, and not attentive enough to its capacity to express love and to build relationships. As a result, a cult of celibacy has developed in which female sexuality, epitomised by Eve, has come to be seen as the greatest threat to godliness. For men, this has meant avoiding contact with women as far as possible, or keeping them in carefully circumscribed roles as virgins, mothers and wives so as to minimise the threat they pose, while denying them any significance in the liturgical and worshipping life of the Church. After all, the female body has no symbolic significance in our worship, since there is no liturgical role that cannot equally be performed by a man. For women, men's fear of sexuality has often meant denying our own bodily capacity for joy and celebration, forcing ourselves to conform to religious and social roles that have been imposed upon us, rather than developing the fullness of our humanity according to our own God-given insights and wisdom. In this climate of denial, negation and fear, sexuality risks becoming so warped that it loses its capacity to unite people together in love, and becomes instead an instrument of power, control and abuse.

Nouwen's image of the wounded Messiah suggests the necessity of both tending to and containing our own sense of being wounded, if we are to minister effectively to others. If we expose all our wounds at once, we become incapacitated and are unable to gather our resources to help others whose needs may be more urgent than our own. But if we keep our wounds permanently covered so that they are never exposed to the healing air, they fester and poison the whole body. We need to learn how to be creative and disciplined in our quest for healing, to know when to speak and when to keep silent, when to bring our grievances into the fresh air of honest dialogue and repentance, and when to cover them for a while in order that we might tend to others.

But beyond the present exposure and pain, this can be a healing process. It is part of a wider transformation in the structures of power and privilege that have for centuries divided the clergy and the laity in a way that prevents the healthy flourishing of communal life. Deference and servility are poor substitutes for genuine authority and respect, and they provide a cover under which abuse multiplies because there are no proper channels of accountability and communication.

The Second Vatican Council was a maturing process in the Church, but such processes take many decades to come to fruition. The acknowledgement of the failures of the past is necessary if the body of the Church is to be healed through the long, slow process of repentance and forgiveness. But there are also signs of healing and growth, particularly in the recent emergence of so many new and vigorous theological voices – the voices of women, of non-western peoples and cultures – suggesting that this is a time of beginnings as well as endings.

One by one, women and priests together must unbind the wounds that have been covered for too long. Women whose children have been abused, women who themselves have been abused, priests whose longing and loneliness have been denied, whose need for love has too often been sacrificed to some discarnate ideal of holiness that is the very antithesis of Christ's example, share this time of suffering. But women can also offer a different way of imagining suffering, one that speaks not of wounding but of bringing to birth. Alongside Nouwen's wounded Messiah, perhaps we need to imagine Mother Church labouring to give birth to the newborn dreams and visions of the pilgrim people of God. All of us, priests and people, men and women, are called to be midwives, to stay with her in her suffering, and to prepare a space of welcome, nurture and warmth for the future struggling to be born among us.

Notes

1. Henri J. M. Nouwen, *The Wounded Healer* (London: Darton, Longman and Todd, 1994), p. xvi.
2. pp. 81–2, quoting the tractate Sanhedrin.

OPEN HANDS

PATRICIA HOWES OSC

Health, in the origin of the word, is to do with wholeness. When I read the words *healing priesthood* in the light of this, a number of memories come to mind, snapshots reminding me that I have experienced the priesthood as a healing ministry. Here I would like to share some of these memories, ways in which priests have ministered the healing of Christ to me, in the hope that my experience may offer pointers to the wider picture.

The first scene is of a group of teenagers on an 'away day' from school, sitting in a circle, talking with two young priests. These priests shared as if we were equals. They listened when we spoke. They heard us and accepted us, and they challenged us. I returned home at the end of the day with a sense of the Church as being 'mine'; I chose to belong to this Church.

Next, my memory offers a series of pictures from a school retreat. We were in the Fifth form (fifteen to sixteen years old) and were away for five days at Spode House, in Staffordshire. There were members of staff and the school chaplain, as well as Fr Shanaghan, a White Father who had been invited to help with the retreat, and some of the Dominicans who ran Spode. We prayed together and we helped to prepare the masses, so 'owned' them in a way we could not usually in the parish. One of the talks stands out in my mind. Fr Shanaghan spoke of his work in South Africa. We heard of apartheid as he had experienced it, which was very different from hearing of it on the news. He told us about Catholics who could not attend Mass together without state harassment because of their colour – yet we who sat in front of him were a group of mixed race. We

45

heard of Bantustans and of the experience of a lady who agreed to move to one, thinking there was a house for her to live in, but who arrived to find nothing but a plot of land. Through his sharing we were meeting Catholic social teaching for the first time and were challenged and awakened.

As the years went by and I found myself in a variety of different situations, the memory of Fr Shanaghan remained. He stood with his back to the wall, in the corner of the room, hands held out, telling us that if we wanted to respond as Christ would, then when we found ourselves with our backs to the wall, our response must not be to hit out but to hold out our hands in friendship – and this after all he had shared of truly unjust situations. Mixed in with such profound experiences, the retreat also contained times of fun and laughter, of learning how to play canasta and playing game after game of it, and a long walk in the Derbyshire Dales. We were given a chance to meet people who could be role models for us, who gave us a wider view of the Church than we had had previously. We met a Church which had room for the idealism of youth, were given to understand that we were wanted in the Church and valued for who we were.

My next snapshots are of my husband's illness and of the priests who came to spend time with us, who brought him the Eucharist or said Mass at home for us, of one who rigged up a bell to allow him to call me without getting a sore throat! Time was taken so that both of us could talk, get in touch with our feelings about his illness, our anger with God and each other. They gave us time, simply to share our lives when life was hard.

A few years ago I was very low, life was difficult, to put it mildly. I phoned a priest friend, a Capuchin brother. He listened to me and told me he would come. The next afternoon, he was here with me. We talked for a long time. He gave me absolution and the sacrament of the Sick. I left that room lighter than I had been in a long time. Burdens were lifted, sickness was alleviated, through my brother's love for me and his willingness to respond to my need. The sense of God's love was such that when the sickness did return it did not overwhelm me in the same way. This was very literally *healing priesthood*.

A common thread in this collection of memories is my aware-ness of being accepted, valued. These priests met me where I was, accepted me, shared my journey, whether fleetingly, on an 'away day', or over an extended period. They gave to me and allowed me to give to them; meals were shared, walks taken, both celebrations and sorrows were shared. These were men of prayer, God-centred, and it was as natural for them to take time to share with me/us in prayer as in other things. They were Christ-like, for this was how Jesus was with people, and people responded, often by deep conversion. Our Lord is incarnate. He became a human being, lived life as we do, in a concrete time and place. He called his disciples, journeyed with them, taught them, ate with them and relaxed with them, and it is in all these different ways that we need our priests to be with us today, as we need them to allow us to minister to them on occasion.

As a postscript I would like to mention one area of priestly ministry where it is easy to give a message contrary to the accep-tance which opens us to the presence of Christ: language. 'Men', 'brothers' and 'sons' are all groups of people I, and half the human race, cannot find myself included in. If used in the liturgy (as when a priest chooses to use Eucharistic Prayer 4 without adapting it), then language is there as a barrier to struggle over. To be accepted, valued, included: these are gifts the Lord gave and which the priest can mediate, and something as simple as language can help or hinder this.

'PROPHETS OF A FUTURE NOT OUR OWN' [1]

CHRISTINE (ALLEN) DENCH

We live in a broken world, marred by poverty and division. It's not a cliché; it means that too many people face a struggle to survive every day. More than a billion people live on less than a dollar a day. Responding to this need is an integral part of the ministry of many priests and religious. In many areas, it is the religious congregations who provide the services (especially health and education). It is common for a parish to be the focal point for community-based services, not just sacramental programmes.

I am talking about very real healing in the face of brokenness, but does this challenge a sense of priesthood, or does it make it more real? This is a short reflection on my experience of knowing and working with priests who are missionaries from European countries living in very poor communities in Latin America.

Priests say that the reality of living in these communities affects any Gospel reading, prompting a call to action. As in the UK, it isn't unusual for parishes to be involved in a variety of social programmes when surrounded by need. But in the likes of a shanty town in Peru they are dealing with everyday survival – community kitchens, health centre, home care networks, work-shops, libraries, etc. They are also involved in wider-ranging projects – national campaigns on HIV awareness, supporting human rights for migrant workers or linking in to political or lay networks on social policy. For them, there is not just the need for an immediate response, but a long-term challenge – towards what *Populorum Progressio* referred to as authentic human development.[1]

Yet even surrounded by poverty, there are those who say it is not for the church to be involved in these activities. And some areas are highly sensitive, for instance around HIV prevention. Dealing with one's colleagues who don't see the same kind of mission can be very draining and frustrating. A key point, however, is about how one responds to the need. A good model for me is one where the need is a catalyst for community effort, not just a matter of an individual's goodness or ego. So it's not a question of having 'Father's projects'.

It is not the role of the priest to be the builder, service provider or even director. From my experience, the successful and appropriate model for the priest is one of facilitation: the person providing the inspiration, motivation and reflection processes for a community response to need. Not the greatest single social activist. The priests I am thinking of admit to struggling with the difference. But, through their own reflection (and in sharing with others), they see how social action can enable people to see it as part of and integrated with their faith, not separate from it. The sort of activity, therefore, that can deepen faith through reflection, and be nurtured by it. It can be a profound faith experience for all involved.

But being the facilitator can be quite different from most priests' original training experience. They were trained for leadership, that is, for being in charge. Here, they have to play a different sort of leadership role – one that enables other people to take on projects, without controlling where they will end up.

All of these missionary priests also had a strong lay team – in fact they had many! Lay people would be running the social pastoral, with the priest being openly supportive and drawing on the experience of the social activity in the Mass – very often relating that experience to the readings. Making faith come alive through action and deepening action through faith. Such reflection on the activity makes the difference between mission and activism. Obviously it is not just something the priest can do. But he has a vital role in providing the sort of reflection that supports those involved in the activity, in deepening their faith, as well as dealing with criticisms or worse.

I have seen priests actively support lay leadership, not just in social concerns but also in the general life of the parish. There are logistics: in Latin American countries (and elsewhere) the priests have to deal with enormous parishes – 60,000 people is not unusual, often spread out geographically. In one area I went to in Peru, there is one priest, 50,000 people and twelve chapels, so a lay team is necessary for people to have any sort of liturgy. They have liturgy and eucharistic services in between the monthly Mass. The women's groups and youth teams have their own programme of activities.

This sort of development takes time and effort, and a particular role for the priest. Again, there is a need to be supportive and enabling, characterised by letting go of the traditional role. This for me is *healing priesthood*, healing the pain often caused by authoritarianism and dogma.

It is in this interface between priest and lay people where I have experienced 'healing' taking place for both lay people and priests. I have seen and experienced lay people enabled to recognise our collaborative role as actors and contributors on this joint venture. I have also seen priests being supported by lay people, avoiding the isolation, depression and exhaustion that is so common.

For me, priesthood is about guiding and supporting a team of lay people in fulfilling the practical and spiritual needs of a local community. In thinking about the experience I have encountered, what has been most healing has been that activity which is joint, participative – and where people have put faith into action. It hasn't been bogged down in ritual or hierarchy, but has been full of respect. It's the kind of priesthood to which we are all called.

In the words of Mgr Oscar Romero of San Salvador, 'We are

workers, not master builders, ministers not messiahs. We are prophets of a future not our own.'[2]

Notes

1. *Populorum Progressio*, 1967.
2. Oscar Romero; 'Prayer for Those in Ministry', 1980.

NO LONE RANGERS

VICKY COSSTICK

To heal means to make whole, and indeed holy. It means to reconnect what is wounded or broken. To be healthy and holy is to be connected to – in right relationship with – God, one's own true self, the earth and the world, our fellow human beings, and the Church, experienced daily as community and tradition, the Gospel and the person of Jesus Christ. This passage summarises Paul's vision of healthy Christian living:

> It is Christ who gave apostles, prophets, evangelists, pastors and teachers roles of service for the faithful to build up the body of Christ, till we become one in faith and in the knowledge of God's Son, and form that perfect man who is Christ come to full stature.
>
> Let us, then, be children no longer, tossed here and there, carried about by every wind of doctrine that originates in human trickery and skill in proposing error. Rather, let us profess the truth in love and grow to the full maturity of Christ the head. Through him the whole body grows, and with the proper functioning of the members joined firmly together by each supporting ligament, builds itself up in love. (Eph. 4:11–16)

What are the implications of this passage for *healing priesthood*? The first point is familiar: Paul envisages a variety of ministries co-operating in service of the growth of the whole community. The community is led by the person of Christ; the aim of Christian life is growth to maturity; the fullness (*pleroma*) of maturity is defined as a Christ-like commitment to truth and love.

In Paul's vision, faith, growth to maturity and knowledge of the truth are essentially interrelated and revolve around the person of Christ. No one is excluded from this journey, although some are called to help others and the whole community on their way. A childish faith is not good enough for anyone. If any ministry is distinguished from the others it is by a greater call to serve, by a deeper understanding and experience of the call to faith, maturity and knowledge.

Paul's language and imagery speak of an organic system. The community, which itself is continually growing, forming, being built up, is made up of individuals who themselves are continually growing and being formed. Perfection in Christ is not fully achievable in this life for any human being. May I suggest that a healthy view of ministry sees it as part of this growing, dynamic, interconnected body-system of the Church?

We can choose whether to stress the set-apartness of the ordained priesthood, or its connectedness. To see priesthood and the Church as an organic system means that ordained priesthood is never an individualistic enterprise, disconnected from community, diocese, bishop, parish or fellow Christian, whether ordained or lay. There are no lone ranger ministries.

At one extreme, ordained priesthood is seen as set apart, eternal, after the order of Melchizedek – a problematic image. From this viewpoint, all aspects of the life of the priest are seen as separate from that of lay Christians. The ordained priest must be formed entirely separately, dress differently, relate closely only to other priests. In recent times, this difference has sometimes been described as 'ontological' – even though John Paul II has only used this word of the priesthood of the whole baptised people of God.[1] The service given by this set-apart priesthood is seen almost exclusively as ritual and sacramental. The fossilised structure of the seminaries has institutionalised such set-apartness.

In my experience, this view of ordained priesthood is not

healthy for priests themselves, nor for the Church as a whole. It can leave the priest disconnected from the gradual, ordinary, stumbling human journey of growth towards a Christ-like maturity to which all baptised Christians are called.

I believe that the fragmentedness of clerical structures (which actually echoes the fragmentedness of postmodern society) has allowed clerical abuse of various forms. A disconnected, dysfunctional structure for selection and formation of clergy will inevitably shelter and collude with disconnected, dysfunctional priests. Time and again, in the unravelling stories of abusing clergy, it can be seen that the set-apartness of the clerical system protected and colluded with the abusive behaviour of clergy, and denied and excluded the experience of victims – who have been treated as wholly *other*, both object and threat.

Paul's vision of the Church as a body makes it clear that we can choose, rather, to understand the community of faith, served by its multiplicity of ministries, as necessarily interconnected and interdependent. With our distinct roles and gifts, we lean on one another and build one another up. To build one individual up, as a believing, knowing, acting Christian does not require putting another down. To nurture one ministry does not require suppressing another. Christian life is not like an enclosed room in which there is not enough oxygen and we must fight one another to breathe. We do not live in an either/or but a both/and world – and Church. Rather, through love and grace, the capacity of every individual and ministry, and the life of the community as a whole is enhanced by mutual support and interconnectedness.

If we see church and ministry as an organic, interconnected, dynamic system, then all aspects of formation are necessarily seen as interrelated. Theological, scriptural, spiritual, pastoral, human and psychological – all are interwoven. The seminary cannot be seen as set apart from the dynamic, evolving life of the wider church community it serves. Further, lay and clergy formation are seen as interconnected. What is common to lay and ordained in the vision of St Paul is greater and more significant than what divides us.

Note
1. See e.g. *Redemptor Hominis* 21.

PART 2

~

VOICES OF WOMEN IN THE PEWS

We are a diverse and in many ways disunited parish, as are probably all parishes, but our very disunity is at the heart of our *healing priesthood*. Many people representing a huge range of cultures, languages, class and political backgrounds come together to worship. Often we do not understand each other, even when we speak the same language. Our interests are so different; our interpretations of the gospel and what it means to live a Christian life also vary enormously. Some of us live very comfortably in financial security and have control over our lives, whilst others have very little control and barely survive financially. It is not unusual for a parent from our church to go hungry so that her child eats well and has the fare to travel to school the next day. These differences often create barriers between us; we avoid people we think don't share the same interests as us, we avoid people we believe hold political views which offend us. All too often we remain within the boundaries of our own cultural, political and class groups, preferring the safety of the familiar to the challenge of uncertainty.

Yet this disunity, which it is essential we challenge, creates the environment within which healing can take place and within which we all play a part. We are unified in our Christianity, expressed in differing ways and circumstances. Our individual sensitivities, gifts and interests pooled are the strength of our community.

Our strength emerges from our differences, and together we are the healing priesthood.

Clare Williams and Marie-Madeleine Savitzky

⁓

Word and Sacrament

How wonderfully are the sacraments moments to remember when there is a real effort on behalf of the priest to welcome people and to understand their faith story. The touch involved in the sacraments can help to convey the healing touch of Christ if these gestures are sensitively administered.

Time spent on carefully preparing homilies is easily detected by members of the congregation. Opportunities to make comments on the homily could help the priest to find out whether his words have conveyed the healing message of Christ.

Meeting deeper needs

All of us need to take time to reflect on our deeper needs. These include assessment of our personal growth, reflecting on how we managed in difficult situations, dealing with moments of sadness and loneliness and failed relationships. Many different persons interact to meet these deeper needs and provide the basis for healing and growth. Priests too have the same human needs. Quality relationships and special friendships are the necessary foundation for healing life's hurts.

Listening

These days we hear about 'listening skills'. Courses abound for us to acquire these listening skills. We all know how wonderfully healing it can be when someone really listens to our story. Priests spend a good proportion of their time listening to others. How often do they find times when in turn they are the ones to tell their story? Unconditional positive regard is a term often used as the quality of a good listener. To be a balanced person we all need to find ways to be in turn the listener and the one who tells her/his story.

Leisure

Stress is the enemy always present in our present style of living in the western world. It is real wisdom to take time off, to enjoy leisure pursuits and to plan relaxing holiday times. All those in the 'caring professions' find it hard to choose wisely about use of leisure time. Parishioners will be pleased when their priests take good care of themselves in this respect.

Retirement

There is a time for giving up full-time work and leaving it to others. Even in an age of shortage of priests there is a right time to say goodbye to work. There are other delights in store for us in our golden years. Retirement holds time and place for healing the wounds of life. Perhaps there are words of appreciation for priests who continue in active ministry till they die on the job. Some years of a quiet life are a gift from God which contribute to our growing old gracefully.

Maureen Farrell FCJ

~

I pray that priests in their role as confessor will receive a fresh, healing breath of the Holy Spirit. Catholic women need to let what is broken be mended. Jesus, drawing life from the Father, forgives us as he forgave the woman caught in adultery; our priests are channels of this healing. They need their own personal Pentecost to be true women's liberators, as Jesus was to our scriptural sisters.

We are mind, soul, spirit and body. A spiritual thirst underlies our daily routine. I've been blessed in recent years to meet priests who have discerned how the lives of Martha and Mary are re-enacted in our own. These inspirational men have nudged me to seek the Lord in every situation. I am learning not to be 'distracted with all the serving' but to serve with love, while making time to sit at his feet.

Truly, a meeting with the living Lord.

Sheila Jacob

~

At the core of this contribution is the relationship of the priest to the parish; a subheading might therefore be 'Parish Priest or Priest to the Parish'. The insufficient number of priests is a separate topic. However, the role of laity and/or attached Sisters to a parish is relevant.

Some argue that the true and essential role of a priest within a parish is to celebrate the sacraments. With or without intent, the running of parishes is increasingly in the hands of laity; leadership differs when a priest has an intimate role and relationship with the parish.

A priest's perceived strengths and priorities may result in excessive time on diocesan tasks. Inevitably, parishioners will experience some lack of 'personal touch'; clerical leadership may result in parishioner frustration. A Parish Council will not necessarily resolve the situation when a priest offers little more than Mass most days and 'is around at weekends'.

A priest's priority is to the parish or the diocese; both bishop and priest need to clarify this. To be a 'parish priest' is to put the spiritual welfare of all age groups and opportunities for spiritual growth second only to sacramental celebration. A 'priest to a parish' is, in my view, unable to achieve this by being too frequently away from the parish, whatever the value of this external involvement. [The same applies to bishops!]

Annette Stapleton

∾

Priests, like everyone else are part of the earth community, dependent upon God's gifts, from rain and sunshine, to bread and wine and the micro-organisms in the soil.

Modern cities make a huge impact on their own and distant environments by using most of the planet's resources of food, timber, metals and fossil fuels and causing most of the pollution. There will be no sustainable world without sustainable cities.

Just a small project around the presbytery or church could make a difference to a priest's environment and send out ripples that others can follow: improved insulation reduces fuel bills for the parish and greenhouse gas emissions for the planet; chiselling out some concrete or rolling back asphalt allows the planting of a tree; a vegetable bed provides recreation and relaxation. A few moments in the open air to think, while uprooting the odd weed, or picking a tomato, plus some really fresh food added to the diet, can't be bad.

A priest who walks or cycles around the parish whenever possible will be fit, a visible and accessible ambassador for Christ to the community and an example of good environmental practice.

Priests need time away from the presbytery, to relax away from the phone, the fax and the overloaded inbox. Whether spending hours in an airport departure lounge and plane is relaxation, is questionable. Aeroplanes are even more climate-damaging than cars. A walking holiday in Wales could prove more rejuvenating than lying on a beach in the Canaries. A train journey under the Channel opens the doorway to the varied cultural delights and cuisines of Europe.

A priesthood centred on a eucharistic and ascetic spirit of gratitude for God's world, and restraint in consuming its gifts could lead to a healthy priesthood and the healing of God's earth.

Barbara Echlin, Christian Ecology Link

~

Thought-provoking words!

Healing: involves recognising the malady, change and renewal.
Priesthood: all Christians share in the common priesthood of Christ through baptism, with a duty to witness to the gospel. A specific ministerial priesthood is conferred by Holy Orders: ordained ministers are called to preach and teach the Word of God, celebrate the Eucharist and sacraments, and have pastoral care for the community entrusted to them. They are given this service in Christ, from whom they receive the necessary graces; this includes the power of healing.

Healing priesthood, then, affects both priests and people.

For me, the priest represents Jesus, walking with us on our faith journey. Priests like everyone, have talents and failings; in knowing themselves, they can show to us the compassionate face of God. Priests who fail to be good role models hurt not just their community, but the whole Church, more especially their brother priests.

Pope John XXIII convened Vatican II to look at how new life could be breathed into the Church. Recognising the need for renewal, he referred us to the early Church: as people learned about Jesus, they began to live what they heard, they shared possessions and homes, gave alms, and cared for each other in living faith. As the Church grew, it acquired many rites, rules and practices that were changed, scrapped and even reintroduced!

The Church today continues to renew itself through liturgical change, and the sharing of certain ministries by lay people. Priests sometimes remain autocratic, but there are also lay people reluctant to get involved and willing to be spoon-fed!

St Peter says, 'Each one, as a good manager of God's different gifts, must use for the good of others the special gift he has received from God' (1 Pet. 4:10–11). The apostles risked being sidetracked from their prime purpose of mission, but when friction arose over the fair distribution of alms, they chose reliable men, laid hands on them invoking the Holy Spirit and delegated this duty to them (Acts 1:1–4). The ordination of married deacons is also a sign of healing taking place.

I think our priests do a fantastic job, especially older priests, who have seen most change and therefore been more challenged. As Christians we have a duty to support our priests. We expect them to be sensitive, welcoming and forgiving. Let us in turn offer them the warmth of true friendship and respect. May we be joyful in our loving service to God through one another, priests and people working together, healing each other.

Joan Salt

∼

Women in the Church today have discovered a lot about what the hierarchy had thought about them – e.g. the terrible prayer known as 'churching' – the purifying of a woman after giving birth said over them after the birth of a baby. It is pure faith in Jesus, who did not condemn women, which keeps us within the Catholic Church today: and faith in the Holy Spirit to change attitudes of those in power and high places in religion.

It is true that mothers encourage and teach their children in the ways of faith more so than fathers who may work all hours of the day. Look around at the congregation; there are more women than men in church.

Celibacy is a beautiful gift to God. It is still very sad that those who fall in love and wish to marry have to leave their vocation. What a waste! It will really be good when we are all equal in our churches as we are in the eyes of God.

Maura Palmer, a Catholic mother

~

The Church recognises that diverse ministries are needed; not all can be left to the ordained priesthood. Many laity have been infantilised; we are to be active not passive (Rom. 8:15). Baptism is the door to all ministry, where we meet as equals. St Augustine said, 'For you I am a Bishop; with you I am a Christian.' We all share responsibility for healing the world; we do not assist, we participate together, recognising each other's gifts.

Pat Kennedy

~

How Priesthood Heals

The very presence of a priest can bring a form of healing, especially to older people, who welcome him as a representative of Christ. For people who are ill or lonely, he may bring something that a lay eucharistic minister cannot. Nevertheless, if his approach is too perfunctory, even traditional Catholics may feel deprived. Priests need to realise they should greet people as individuals. Their words may carry a special quality which lends to their statements a conviction which has the potential to heal – or indeed to damage.

Implications

Consequently both the initial and the in-service training of priests should familiarise them with appropriate ways of compassionate and personal ministry. They should also be up to date with scripture scholarship, as they may be thought more qualified to speak for the Church than lay people.

How Priesthood Needs to Be Healed
Selection
- Potential priests should be psychologically mature (especially if celibacy is still to be imposed).
- Potential priests need to be open to new ideas, and flexible in approach.
- Potential priests need a reasonable level of education, such as a university degree or equivalent, or experience in a demanding job.

(I consider that the admission of women and married men would bring healing to the priesthood.)

Training
- Priests need help in developing qualities such as empathy.
- Seminaries should allow students to live outside, either with their own families or in shared accommodation.
- Students should go away for their annual retreat.
- Seminary professors should have academic qualifications equivalent to university teachers; non-graduate seminarians should be able to accumulate degree credits.
- Seminarians should spend some time working with students for non-Catholic ministries.
- Courses should include contributions from non-Catholic

and non-Christian religious experts, and opportunities for shared worship.
- Courses should include work in areas of social deprivation.
- Familiarity with the spiritual classics from all sources should be encouraged.

Compulsory In-service Courses
- Regular weekly or summer-school courses to familiarise clergy with developments in Scripture, theology, psychology, counselling, sociology, etc.
- An extended period of study leave after a fixed period of years, or the opportunity for relevant visits abroad.

Involvement of Lay People
- Well-qualified people of both sexes should be fully involved at all levels of training.
- Greater parish involvement of lay people, who may have more expertise than priests in giving sermons, chairing committees, conducting services and house visiting. More education is needed to help parishioners welcome the ministrations of lay people in such roles.

(Dr) Pat Pinsent, Senior Research Fellow

Other contributors not specifically included here made similar points.

From the core of my being, I long for the priests in our Church to have healthy training in interpersonal relationships. Priests take the vow of celibacy: that does not mean that they are not responsible for engaging in healthy interpersonal relationships with people in their parishes, yet the number of priests who are able to offer friendship, in particular to women, are sadly very few and far between. Priests give directions and wield their power, but rarely are they willing to be vulnerable enough to offer any sense of connectedness; not only are we excluded from knowing who they are, but they do not put energy into coming to know who we are. So we often get homilies that have nothing to do with us but are from the priest's agenda. Yes, of course, I am exaggerating because one can come across a priest who is open to being befriended, but this, in my experience, is the exception, not the norm. Seminaries seem to prepare them for the academics of their vocation but not for engagement with the people of God, so the priest's ability to effect change and growth in people's faith-journey is very limited. An honest commitment to developing skills for handling interpersonal relationships would certainly aid healing the priesthood.

Linda Conroy

~

God will heal in his way, in his time; we can be his vessels to show how much he loves us and wants us to love him.

The sacraments of the Sick, Reconciliation and the Eucharist can be almost 'sterile occasions' – rituals devoid of compassion and love, words and actions but from closed ears and empty hearts, priests keeping people at arm's length or with feet planted high on elevated altars. No gentle touch, no relationship, no compassion, no care: elitist behaviour, reminiscent of the Pharisees in Jesus' time.

Yet God sent Jesus to show us the way, through love and relationship, and the power of the Holy Spirit. Jean Vanier in *Tears of Silence* says compassion means sharing the same passion, suffering . . . agony. In order to understand what another person is experiencing, we have to open our minds and hearts to their experience, to listen and try to understand them. This demands encounter, just like the risen Jesus walking alongside the disciples on the road to Emmaus.

In encountering others at a deep level, in allowing their pain and suffering to touch us, we also get to know ourselves. We become the person God wants us to be. We have to be vulnerable to grow and, in so doing, healing becomes a reciprocal process. We are all called to the healing priesthood.

Angela Tyson

~

When the word 'priesthood' is mentioned, a stereotypical picture springs to mind of a group of middle-aged black-clad men, aloof, overbearing, powerful, status-bound, inward-looking, unsympathetic, sexist, set apart from the community, condemnatory, living in the past, or wishing they could. This impression of the priesthood as a whole is the product of having belonged to the Church for nearly sixty years; of belonging to parishes where the priest is regarded as the only adult and wants to keep it that way; where respect and obedience are demanded because of the office, no matter how badly the person who holds the office behaves, and all this in a strange atmosphere of fear. It is as if going against the opinion of a priest on ordinary everyday organisational matters is going against God himself.

When I think of individual priests, the picture is different. It is one which evokes sympathy and concern. I see priests in one-man parishes, who are lonely, confused and unsupported. Those who have not received or not realised the need for training in the various areas of the work they are trying to do, are feeling failures or disillusioned. Many have to bear the brunt of laity unrest and falling numbers and people are looking to them for leadership. The lives they lead do not enable priests to understand how ordinary people live in the world. In my experience, people tell them what they want to hear; they are surrounded by 'yes' people.

Change has to be managed carefully for fear of offending some people.

What can be done? Here are some suggestions:

- a report clarifying the role of the priest and implementation of recommendations
- training in management and interpersonal skills for all priests
- ongoing in-service training
- opportunity to keep in touch with the challenge of non-ordained life
- deep reflection on forms of priestly ministry, in the light of Vatican II
- priests to be accountable, to bishop and laity
- laity given training and responsibility in parishes, working with, not for, the priest.

Anon

These points are representative of other contributors.

∼

There are two aspects to this issue: we need a different kind of clerical leadership if it is to be relevant in today's changed conditions; and the ordained priesthood can be a medium of healing – not just through new forms of the sacrament of Reconciliation. The two, however, are inextricably mixed.

Desirable Qualities of the Ordained Priest

A prayerful person, able to inspire and empower others, friendly and approachable, a searcher for truth, humble and compassionate, eschewing authoritarian approaches. Counselling should be available for priests, and also adequate in-service training, so that skills in interpersonal relationships, personal awareness and team leadership can be developed (see the Bishops' publication, *The Sign We Give* (1996), on collaborative ministry). Where bishops are concerned, they need training in managerial techniques so as to inspire their priests more effectively.

Liturgy

Efforts should be made to meet the varying needs of people in the parish, e.g. children's masses, occasional youth vigils, house masses, as well as the usual Eucharists in the parish church. Priests should be aware of the alienating effect of addressing women as 'brethren' and instead use phrases such as 'pray brothers and sisters', which is a permitted variation. Women and girls should be encouraged as altar servers, readers, collectors, etc. (the ban on discussing the issue of ordaining women should be lifted: women have great gifts to offer ministry).

Prayer

Active steps should be taken to deepen the prayer life of the faith community.

Ecumenism

It is helpful if the priest recognises the importance of this, is actively involved and encourages the people.

Mrs I. Pratt

My experience of healing through reconciliation started in 1964, when at sixteen I first received the sacrament face to face, instead of from a disembodied voice behind a grille. Over the years I found that the more open the priest has been about sharing his own experience as well as listening to me opening my heart, the more healing has been the sacrament. No automaton, but a fellow-sinner who knows God's love and forgiveness. The touch of his hands on my head at the words of absolution and the hug of encouragement for me and thanks for him make the forgiveness tangible.

I experienced healing too while I was anointed during a bad depressive episode and especially when I had my feet washed and kissed one Maundy Thursday.

The more priests open themselves to their parishioners as

ordinary human beings who come from a family, with a past life of education, work and friendship which shaped their character, and are still growing and developing, the more we can see them as examples of God's love to emulate, celebrate and support.

They cannot live in the sheltered clerical vacuum of yesterday from seminary to presbytery to cemetery. They often live alone with no one to talk to about the good and bad parts of the day. Unless parishes are reorganised so that several priests live together and go out to work in their parishes, they will need to have a confiding relationship with some parishioners or risk their mental health.

Has there been any research into whether married priests (orthodox or ex-Anglican) or those living in groups, have more or less depression, burn-out, alcoholism or deviant sexual behaviour than those who live alone?

Val Vardon

Now a single parent and mother of a large, extended family, my journey in faith began with the premature birth of my first child. Against all health adversities these child-bearing years relied heavily on devotion to my Catholic faith, and respect for the priesthood as 'advocate and spiritual healer'. At times, I felt sadly let down by a faith that did not practise what it preached!

While I believe the majority of priests do encourage confidence and spirituality, some seem to have an 'ivory tower' philosophy and need to consider carefully our common humanity in Christ.

The family is the nucleus of the Church, and true vocations arise from this. The nature of vocations whether for men or women, including the role of motherhood in the Church, depends upon a healthier outlook and insight sought from the Church as a whole. Without this, there will be fewer and weak vocations.

Media publicity about abusive priests has sent shock waves through the whole Catholic community, the aftermath resulting in innocent priests being targeted, intimidated and victimised, and their confidence shattered. They can be assured of our prayers and support, for if blame is to be apportioned we must all take our share!

What is the Church's role?

1. Provide help and support for both innocent and perpetrator priests.
2. Prioritise research into vocation and Catholic family life.
3. Make the Liturgy inclusive: 'man and woman', 'people', etc.

We need to reflect upon our common humanity and make space to grow together in fullness.

Pauline Ryan

~

We ourselves are the *healing priesthood* – a people who extend Christ's healing touch to each other as we witness to the kin(G)dom of God. Jesus' birth announced the year of God's favour and its sign was to hear the Good News, to be healed, and for injustice to be ended. Jesus was in the line of prophets who proclaimed the compassionate love of God for God's priestly people and who spoke out against vested interests and a post-exilic errant priesthood. Jesus was the awaited intervention of God foretold by Malachi, creating in himself a renewed priesthood to offer sacrifice which would be 'pleasing to God, as in the days of old ' (Mal. 3:4). Jesus' compassionate healing pointed beyond the healing and revealed God's true way of seeing. This challenged the status quo and so Jesus was killed. We are baptised prophet and priest in Christ Jesus; that healing power we receive points beyond, challenging the blindness in our own times. Helder Camara said, 'When I say the poor have no bread they call me a saint; when I ask why the poor have no bread they call me a communist' (*Sister Earth*, 1996) – and his prophetic words live on. When women help the housebound and take communion to the sick they are commended; when they ask why they may not consecrate that Bread they are contradicted, but their

inclusion in this priestly gift from Jesus Christ is a sign of the
kin(G)dom. Baptised as Christ-prophet-priest we are moved by
the Spirit, while the healing power of our word makes God
present to the world and points to the year of God's favour.

Dr Jacqueline Field-Bibb

❧

The leadership of the priest considerably influences the attitude
of the congregation. With one notable exception, priests I have
known do not wish to become involved in broken personal
relationships. I have also encountered one who sought to fulfil
his brokenness in ways incompatible with celibacy.

'Bear one another's burdens' – women are very good at this,
given opportunity and encouragement.

Diane Robertson

❧

The parish community needs to be aware of and involved with
the whole community. My experience has been that without
active dedicated women many parishes would struggle to survive. It is women who are catechists, Eucharistic ministers,
scripture readers, St Vincent de Paul members, social workers
visiting the elderly/sick at home and in hospital, and fund-
raisers. I feel that women with vocations could be ordained as
deacons and further their work in parishes.

I have become aware that there is very little help/support
given to those who are single parents, either through divorce or
other circumstances. Many are struggling with marital problems; there should be someone in the parish whom they could
talk to. Priests cannot be available to everyone, but it is essential
that the parish has an appointed person to meet these needs.

Is the Church listening to women? I have not heard of any
initiatives in our deanery.

E. Jennings

❧

First, let's heal priesthood, before we help it to be more healing.
- there needs to be: better initial discernment, by both candidates and authorities; different types of training – candidates should live among the people, and go to seminary on day or evening release; they need time for and guidance in prayer, pastoral work and use of leisure, but not in a hothouse atmosphere.
- part-time ordained or fixed-term ministry should be options, perhaps more than once in a person's life. If the Christian vocation is all of a piece, then people can be called for a time to priesthood, just as some are to religious life.
- in chronic shortage, the community should be asked if there is anyone, celibate, married or single who feels called and would be willing to serve for a time in the role of priest. After a period of discernment and training, s/he should be able to take up this position.

A priesthood which is so much healthier in itself will thus be in a better position to heal and minister to others.

Ruth Wood

I was always under the impression that priests, through the power invested in them at ordination, were healing priests; they ministered to our spiritual needs and cured our spiritual ills through the sacraments and the Sacrifice of the Mass.

Great women saints such as St Catherine of Siena and St Teresa of Avila – Doctors of the Church – have influenced popes and changed abuses – but they behaved always with the dignity of women. In former times, if you couldn't live up to the laws of the Church, you left – it was as simple and as honourable as that. So I see absolutely no reason for the clamouring and protesting that goes on among modern-day feminists.

Catherine Reitzik

And in similar vein:

It would seem that the Eucharistic minister is increasingly taking over the duties of the priest. As far as I can see, the only way that the Church can move forward is to move back to those essentials which made our Church strong and flourishing: the traditional Mass, with Latin (that could be understood and followed in English in the Missal); the teaching of the catechism to our children, whereby they would learn the fundamentals of our faith.

Elizabeth King (Mrs)

~

The Church has not always treated women very commendably . . . for whatever reason, we seem to have been regarded as the dangerous sex . . .

Not long after a very messy and protracted ectopic pregnancy, I heard a priest lamenting over those babies lost through abortion. He said they had no way to heaven because they had not been born. This left me confused about the destiny of miscarried or lost babies like my own, or those which unknown to their parents failed to implant in the womb. I have never ceased to mourn my child whose existence I was unaware of until I lost it, and whose sex I will never know. Are priests too embarrassed or ill-informed to discuss these issues?

On another occasion, I read of a priest scoffing at the idea of praying to a guardian angel. The attitude seemed to be 'yes we believed in such things in the 1950s, but we know better now'. How dare he remove the comfort of anyone's belief in such a way? How smug I was when soon after, our Bishop urged us to pray to guardian angels.

Yes, some priests have a lot of healing to do and a lot of 'sorrys' to say. We are not the lesser sex, because in God's eyes we are equal. I am not surprised he entrusted the care of his only son to a woman.

Jacky Matton (Mrs)

~

How fortunate we are that people devote their lives to the Church by ordination. Some thoughts:

- Given modern communications, amazed at amount of time Church takes to make statements and implement decisions, especially on injustices, e.g. six years before girl altar servers allowed in our parish; long delay in the Pope's statement regarding paedophile priests.
- Good news about the Church should be advertised.
- How is the Church as worldwide organisation run? Even on parish level, community's involvement should be encouraged, for instance, committee to oversee five-year plan, including spiritual development. Women's groups try to activate and jostle such involvement; our Ladies' Group organises social and parish events, cleaning and flower arranging rosters, music and liturgy for children.
- Hope for development of 'All Faith' schools.

Anon

∼

The training of priests is still geared to a situation in state and Church which no longer pertains. Taking men out of their families and societies contributes to their rootlessness. The myriad social costs paid by priests are known to everyone.

There have been too many reflection papers, discernment seminars, depositions, submissions, petitions – all to no avail. A calendar of meetings has to be set up with a clear aim for change. As long as priests are not accountable to their communities, you will have a two tier-system, priests and 'laity' – a word altogether difficult to accept nowadays, because it means 'the uneducated masses' originally. As long as there are 'priests', who are the only ones who can dispense sacramental power, there will be the second-class 'everybody else' who is not termed 'priest'. We need to be serious about the 'priesthood of all people', the sharing of gifts, talents.

We need to aim for a renewed understanding of what is church, what is this community's role in everybody's life. To me it is not a question of healing priesthood, but of healing the rift that exists as long as there is a priesthood over and above all those who are not termed 'priests'.

The Church has alienated women for far too long. Young women are by and large no longer interested in organised religion. Young men, to judge by the lack of those training for the priesthood, are no longer interested either. We do not need to bother about 'priesthood'; we need to set out to reform what we term *community*, that is, the meaning – the original meaning – of *church*.

dmcewan

~

Christ did not formally ordain anyone, but called people to be his followers. Worship, in the time of Christ, followed the line of Jewish table fellowship, often in the homes of women, with leadership provided by both men and women. Besides the twelve apostles, women also travelled with Jesus. Luke (8:1–3) speaks of Mary Magdalene, Joanna and Susanna as some of the women following and supporting Jesus' ministry.

Mary Magdalene features in all four resurrection accounts. The proclamation of the resurrection rests upon her testimony.

Mary, Jesus' mother, cared for him through childhood and was with him through his death and resurrection. She truly ministered to Christ.

The priesthood and Eucharistic worship did not fully resemble what we know until the fourth century.

We all need each other. Our various gifts need to be shared so that all our lives may be enriched.

Mary Weetman

~

My understanding of priesthood has come through a long and interior struggle to understand the call, a struggle that involved years of frustration, as I had no one to turn to for help or under-standing. It involved some bitterness and anger; I was sure I would have found all the necessary help, encouragement and understanding if I had been male rather than female. The ques-tion was how to exercise my priesthood in the way I could, rather than in the way I couldn't. Time and prayer taught me the following:

It seemed to me that priesthood had a dual function – a way to knowing Christ and also a way to minister Christ to others.

I was already immersed into Christ – after all I was baptised into Christ as priest, prophet and king. I intuitively realised that it was only a question of time and faithfulness to my journey before this reality (of coming to live wholly in the confidence of God) would blossom into life.

This helped me come to terms with the terrible sense of rejection I felt in the Church's attitude to the ordination of women. I realised that the function of the parish priest goes beyond priestly function. The Church's understanding of priesthood seems to be also tied up with the idea of pastoring, preaching and governance. It seems to me that this under-standing can only be classified as priesthood if it brings love, confidence, and growth to people. All these functions are not exclusively the work of the ordained.

Priesthood is a way of life that is open through prayer. A priest is a person of prayer. Time spent daily in exclusive and attentive prayer helps us open up to the power of God's Spirit, a Spirit that is healing and freeing, as we grow in self-knowledge and confidence in God's love. All is gift and everything comes at the appropriate time.

Our ministering Christ to others is also gift as we go about our lives in the openness of prayer and confidence that love always raises up what needs to be raised up. Our prayer becomes one lived with Christ in the continual intercession of

'Father, may they all be one, may they be one in us, as you are in me and I am in you.'

Mrs C. Gamson

~

Priesthood is at present wounded and weak. There is a serious need for thorough screening, by professional psychologists, of all applicants, especially in view of the continued demand for permanent celibacy, which is neither biblical, nor upheld in the early Church; celibacy is a gift for the few.

The traditional role of the priest was one of authority, governing, teaching, needing to be revered. Today, as 'Servant to All', the priest needs to look for and use all the talents of willing parishioners, enabling a 'People's Parish'.

As shepherd, the priest needs good scriptural knowledge for meaningful community prayer and sermons, and concern for ongoing instruction for young people, so that school-leaving does not mean church-leaving.

As healer, he needs to plan Reconciliation services that bring peace to those attending. Maybe the actual confessing of sins at this service could be optional.

During my long life as a religious, about nine priests have helped me in times of special need. I could relate to them as healers and guides because they related to me as a woman and respected me. They listened attentively, did not talk down, accepted my personality and experience and were not afraid to challenge me.

The Church has made some effort to listen to women. Some clergy use inclusive language, important to women who have felt excluded by the continual use of 'man'. Another area is sensitive provision for women in Reconciliation. It is difficult and embarrassing for a woman to confess sexual sins to a man; some find it impossible. Women would welcome General Absolution without actual confessing of these sins. When necessary, those who wish could use a 'proxy' – another woman who would 'hear' their confession and repeat it to a priest for absolution.

The teaching, caring Church seems unaware of the extent of domiciliary violence. Twenty per cent of women suffer physical abuse at home, but do we ever hear a sermon condemning this behaviour? Are priests given training on how to get men to face, admit and control violent behaviour? Yet advice is readily given by priests on Natural Family Planning, which can itself place strain on a relationship. The Church fails to understand and respond to women.

Success stories, however, include the transformation of a parish by a Parish Sister; the admission of altar girls, and women as Eucharistic Ministers. Parish Councils include women, though the parish priest often makes the decisions.

There are women theologians, but women are rarely asked to preach; women hold responsible jobs in government and business, but are rarely involved in parish consultations; women form the majority in congregations, but mainly function as tea-ladies, cleaners, etc. We are grossly underused and under-estimated.

Women have written books highlighting from Scripture the 'feminine' side of God and the sensitivity of Jesus to women and children. I do not hear these prayers or aspects of Jesus being mentioned or emphasised.

My own experience includes nursing, social work, accredited counselling and spiritual direction, followed by further biblical and theological studies. Yet I find that most of my talents and imagination have been used by the Church of Scotland Guilds.

Anon, Scotland

~

Now in my fifties, the 1980s saw me very low, physically, mentally and spiritually. Yet my friends would say I 'had it all' – professional job, lovely family, good looks, etc. Only I knew the emptiness, the physical toil and illness – I did not know the cause.

I heard of 'charismatic' renewal in a chance conversation with a Catholic woman. Later, at an Anglican service, a Catholic priest performed a 'laying on of hands'. I prayed hard: 'Lord, don't let anything happen to me!' But the words prayed over my colleague stayed with me and I went to several more services.

One day, I stumbled across a prayer group, a vibrant, joyful, caring community with a Catholic priest occasionally involved. Numerous little emotional healings began to occur for me. My faith became real. My prayers for others were answered in amazing ways. Slowly, I realised I had changed.

As I matured through reading and prayer, I occasionally met priests who would respond after my confessions to my request, 'Father, I would like a word of knowledge.' Invariably the words of wisdom were right.

I have often seen the Holy Spirit's power manifest through the healing ministry, with laity and priests involved. I understand priests' concern about 'emotionalism', and the possibility of discomfort and embarrassment when onlookers see somebody crying – or even joyful! But it is the ongoing change, witnessed months later, that proves the healing.

Many priests seem reluctant to lay hands on the faithful and pray, to hold an occasional healing service, to give the sacrament of the Sick (unless really ill or dying) or just simply to visit the sick and lay on hands. It is a source of sadness and concern that this incredible gift – given to priests – is so little used or perhaps not even recognised.

I would like to thank the few priests I have encountered who have actively encouraged my faith, prayed with me, and administered the sacraments of Reconciliation and of the Sick. My faith is alive.

Anon

∼

This consultation raised lots of questions for me about my relationship with the present priesthood, so I avoided it. However, I experienced a wonderful retreat at St Beunos in Wales recently and now feel duty bound to respond – but I haven't time to polish it into beautiful prose!

With sadness, I realise I haven't received any significant experience of healing from an ordained priest except for my first confession when a Cambridge university student twenty-one years ago.

I suppose I'm lucky that I haven't had huge crises in my life, but I would only turn to an ordained priest if I have respect for him – I am often unable to see God beyond the person.

So often priests are defensive, set apart by living alone, unable to form warm human relationships, especially with women: this creates a barrier for me.

I probably see priests as authoritarian and gatekeepers, far removed from the gospel view of service. The washing of feet on Maundy Thursday seems an empty ritual, especially when an altar server is delegated to do it. So in this sense, my image of the priesthood definitely needs healing.

I have, however, experienced healing from those, considered by many Catholics to be outside the mainstream Church, who, *despite* their ordination have been whole human beings, full of God's love. My present spiritual journey is fortunately taking me into contact with more of them, so I live in hope.

If you consider that we are all called to be priests by our baptism, then I know we have a healing priesthood: non-ordained people have made me whole again – my husband, my female director on a recent retreat, friends and family, and also the written word, music, art and conventional medicine.

I don't think the Church has a future until the ordained priesthood, open to the healing power of the Holy Spirit, ceases to fear the change needed to walk *with us* and *alongside us*. The love of God is unchanging, but I am sure God wants to be able to speak to people in the here and now – where they are.

I take a personal view here, based on my experience and making sweeping generalisations; I ask God's forgiveness if I have forgotten healing received through ordained priests – and ask for healing of my memory!

I recognise that globally there are many priests who work for healing between communities, for peace and justice in war-torn areas of the world, often putting their own lives on the line – and I give thanks to God for them. But it is in the small one-to-one relationships, that could be classed as trivial when considering the big picture of human suffering, that healing is so desperately needed.

Judith Pollock

PART 3

WOMEN'S VOICES:
INTERNATIONAL

'TALITHA KUM!'[1]

GERALDINE HAWKES

In considering *healing priesthood*, we recognise the great healing ministry of Jesus and recall the many people who called on him and asked for his healing touch. Our Church is in need of healing today in many ways. The relationship between the Church and women is one such area and the healing priesthood of Jesus has much to teach us.

In Australia, during the 1970s to 1990s, the Australian Catholic Bishops received many suggestions and representations from a range of people and groups who were concerned about the role and status of women in the Church.

She came up behind him and touched the fringe of his cloak. (Luke 8:44)

These voices were heard to be calling for the role and status of women to be considered as a matter of social justice and in 1996 the Australian Catholic Bishops Conference launched a research project, the focus of which was the participation of women in the Catholic Church in Australia. The project was a major event for the Catholic community across Australia, and thousands of women and men participated. The process included written submissions, contextual papers, public hearings and meetings with targeted groups.

Then looking up to heaven he sighed; and he said to him, 'Ephphatha,' that is, 'Be opened.' (Mark 7:35)

The research project showed that the dominant feeling of participants was one of pain and alienation. Its major findings were:

1. The active involvement of women in the life of the Church, and in all aspects except for the ordained ministry, is considerable and significantly greater than that of lay men.
2. The roles they fill, however, are secondary, ancillary, and even menial, resulting in feelings of deep pain, anger and alienation.
3. Both women and men are calling for women to have leadership roles and a real voice in the decision-making processes of the Church. Many were of the view that this is only achievable if women are admitted to the ordained ministry.

And everyone in the crowd was trying to touch him because power came out of him that cured them all. (Luke 6:19)

The research identified various barriers to women's participation in the Church, the greatest of which were the patriarchal attitudes and traditions which were seen to be inconsistent with the person and message of Jesus Christ, and failed to take into account developments in the social sciences and changes in the role of women in the wider society.

The structures of the Church were experienced as male-dominated, hierarchical and authoritarian. These authoritarian attitudes, together with the misuse of power and position, were seen as preventing women's participation.

Then he laid his hands on the man's eyes again and he saw clearly. (Mark 8:25)

The key issue arising from the research project was gender equality, recognising the equal dignity of women and men created in the image and likeness of God. The wider Australian society was seen as far more affirming and accepting of the changing role and equality of women than the Church. The need to increase opportunities for women's involvement in decision-making and leadership were constantly named as a major issue.

Following the research, a report entitled *Woman and Man: One in Christ Jesus* was presented to the Australian Catholic Bishops Conference in 1999. The Bishops received this, reflected on it and made their response in September 2000 in the Social Justice Sunday Statement. Here, they described nine decisions for action at the national level and thirty-one proposals for consideration in dioceses across Australia.

And taking the child by the hand, he said to her 'Talitha, kum!' which means, 'Little girl, I tell you to get up.' (Mark 5:41)

One such decision was the establishment of a Commission for Australian Catholic Women whose role is to:

- act as a focal point for ongoing dialogue, theological reflection and pastoral planning on women's participation in the Catholic Church in Australia
- facilitate the implementation of decisions and recommendations arising from the report and contained in the Social Justice Statement.

The Commission recognises that it requires the whole Church to work collaboratively to implement these decisions, which include such diverse aspects as clergy formation, research on the theology of the human person and the integration of elements of indigenous culture into liturgical celebration. It will also take a great commitment and much letting go of power if the Church is to move from current patriarchal attitudes and traditions to a new way of being church which is more at one with the person and message of Jesus Christ.

And if we have the courage to respond to this challenge and seek to be faithful to the model of priesthood as Jesus lived it, perhaps we will be able to better respond to the many needs of our society through becoming individuals and communities which:

- listen and are not judgemental

- are compassionate and aware of our own vulnerability
- are prayerful
- don't always feel that we have to have the answer
- participate in the struggle
- are welcoming of all and make space for others, especially the hidden or small or unspoken
- find joy in discovering and nurturing each other's energy and passion
- share responsibility for the physical and spiritual well-being of individuals, families and communities.

'My daughter,' he said, 'your faith has restored you to health; go in peace and be free from your complaint.' (Mark 5:34)

'HELLO, SR JESUS!'

JOAN MARSHALL

I arrived in North-east Brazil for the first time in 1980. On my way to Mass I was so surprised to hear a little four-year-old girl cry out, 'Hello, Sr Jesus!' and then to her mother, 'Mummy, Mummy, there goes the Church!' Red in the face and feeling very humble, I was stopped in my tracks and began to reflect on the true meaning of my life as a missionary, a follower of Jesus and a sign of the living Church.

The Church today is very aware of the struggle it is engaged in to be sacrament and sign of God's presence in the world. It needs to be the kind of herald that speaks in a familiar language and in thought patterns that people can understand, and the kind of institution that leads as servant. Individual Christians also have the responsibility to be an authentic Gospel sign. We let the light of Christ shine through us to others, assuming the role of prophet, priest and king, embracing all with God's tender compassion.

Having the opportunity to live in Africa and Brazil since 1976 has shown me how unrealisable were the demands made on so many priests to minister alone to parishes of 30,000 and 60,000 parishioners, an impossible feat that has destroyed many and deprived the population of spiritual nourishment. How can we help and heal this ever-growing situation – be more active members of our Church?

The concept of God as Mother and Father is not new. Masculine and feminine images of God abound in sacred Scripture: the fourteenth-century mystic, Julian of Norwich, puts it beautifully in her *Revelations of Divine Love*:

91

A mother's caring is the closest, nearest and surest for it is the truest. This care never might nor could nor should be done fully except by him alone ... Our true mother Jesus, who is all love, bears us into joy and endless living. Blessed may he be!

My years in Brazil and Africa put me in touch with priests who really desired the collaboration of women, who saw the necessity to complete people's understanding of God by reflecting the feminine aspects of God's heart. My experience helped me to understand what it means to be Church.

In Brazil, we lived in a parish with 35,000 parishioners, one priest, a community of four religious and numerous lay helpers – a real team with lots of networking. As in most developing countries, death is so close to us; most weeks we had funeral services and the privilege of sharing with families their time of suffering and grief. How many times have we been called to the bedside of the dying to listen to the outpouring of their hearts? How often have we been begged to give absolution, knowing that the priest was unable to come? With confidence we have been able to reply that our loving and merciful God forgives all.

How many women suffering physical and emotional abuse come to pour out their stories, incapable of doing this with a man! So many people need a listening ear, someone with time to understand their situation and show compassion.

There were also the joys of new births and baptism preparations, where there would be deep sharing with families about their responsibilities in the Christian upbringing of their children, and then the sharing of the Spirit's outpouring during the baptism ceremony and the celebration afterwards.

Other privileged moments for me were the Sunday liturgy preparations, where, with the priest and several lay people, we prepared texts and songs, and together worked on the homily. Each day, Communion services were held in the numerous chapels in different parts of the town. Explanations of the Word of God were carefully prepared by different members of the local community, who often came to our house to use the library and available commentaries. Our priest had a community-making function, not at all authoritarian, but getting people to consider how they could do things together.

In many of our African villages, the people only see the priest once a year, but thanks to the basic communities, each day they can listen together to the Word of God and receive communion, the children can be baptised, the youth can have a deeper Christian formation, adults can prepare for the sacraments, and the dead can have a Christian burial.

Being in community and not alone is not only a life support for the members but also for the wider community. How many people have said to us, 'It's so good just to know that you are there and at any moment we can knock at your door and won't be turned away. We don't feel that we are disturbing you, you are there for us!'

For me, a healing priesthood would be: daring to portray a new face of the Church – small communities who are a presence where others do not go; building the Kingdom, together with the laity in mutual evangelisation; 'restoring the Church' by becoming bridge-builders; opening the way to restore personal dignity to the marginalised and excluded; setting free seeds of new life in our hearts and in the hearts of those to whom we are sent. Thus we would be bearers of and witnesses to hope, daring to live open to the future.

The Church as sacrament presents externally to the world the Jesus who is its head, the love of God active in the world. As members of the Church, we are also sacrament: God is present in the world through us, unworthy disciples. We are his light that shines on others, the salt which gives flavour to the world. We are his hands that do good deeds, his eyes that forgive, his comforting words.

Our task as Church is to be a sign that people understand and recognise. Through our deeds people will recognise the Spirit who is in us. Through us Jesus reveals himself to the world.

Our challenge is to be a sacrament of Jesus Christ!

FROM HEALING TO WHOLENESS[1]

TOOS STARMAN

Priesthood includes more than one aspect:

- priestly mission, in which the priest mediates salvation between God and humankind
- preaching, making heard the message of the gospel
- pastoral care, pastoral and spiritual guidance.

It is healing when all three aspects are involved.

Priesthood that tries to mediate God's rich and multi-coloured care for humankind also heals by bringing completeness. Humans are called by God to become whole, to be helped, to be cured, to thrive, to be saved – the many different words emphasise God's power and work in people. Jesus emanated healing power; the priest is a human mediator of this power. A doctor may be able to cure you, a friend may be able to pull you out of a distressing situation – people can be healing for one another. But in priesthood all these elements converge. Healing means allowing people to live with their past, their shortcomings and potential, body and soul, falling and rising again, in health and in sickness. Priesthood is both sign and symbol of God's healing power. *Healing priesthood* helps people to integrate their life-history, their experiences of joy and sorrow, good and bad action.

Priesthood covers many functions in the service of God's people, so it is good that it is executed by a variety of people, each with her/his own specific possibilities. Unless some elements remain invisible or are forgotten, the totality can show something of God's activity among us. I personally encounter healing priesthood where women and men are complementary in their priestly mission, preaching and pastoral task, in a collaboration through which priesthood is itself healed. I suggest that a priesthood which invites and stimulates all kinds of people to share in it may be called healing priesthood, as in the following examples from my twenty-one years' experience of pastoral work.

A family with two children, one three years old, one four months: I had met the parents, who were non-practising Catholics, when as Pastoral Worker I prepared a close relative for reception into the Church. When their baby died suddenly, the bereaved parents contacted me and asked me to baptise him. I said that baptism is meant for the living. We talked at length, to find out what they were seeking. Their deepest wish was: *God, bless this child. Take it into your Light and help us to bear this suffering.* Together we compiled a funeral service, in which we tried to come to terms with the parting, with space for sorrow and where they could contribute their own words. As a sign of consolation, we lit a baptismal candle from the light of the Paschal Candle: *May this child live in God's eternal light.*

Five years later, they contacted me again. Another baby had been born, but they had gone through very hard times, with bankruptcies and debts and had done a lot of thinking. Now they wanted to refresh their belief in God, in the shape of gratitude for the friendship and solidarity they had met and for the strength to carry on. They wanted both sons to be baptised and their marriage to be brought before God. When I told them I was not allowed to baptise, they were astonished, unable to comprehend. Could it be that I was allowed to conduct a funeral service and bury their dead child but was forbidden to baptise their two living children?

In consultation with a priest-colleague, we found a solution: we applied for church recognition of the marriage, and in this 'emergency situation' I was permitted to baptise the children.

During the baptism we prayed for God's blessing on the marriage.

In this process I experienced healing priesthood, the opportunity to mediate grace in the family's spiritual search. It was important that the whole process be co-ordinated and conducted by one person, essential that the Church's mediator role was made concrete through someone the couple trusted, who knew their history and understood their struggle (rather than start again with someone new). In talking, the couple had integrated their difficult life-experience with the history of God's relationship with his people. They found coherence – it made sense, was healing for them; we felt that it was good. At the same time, care was taken that the family's relationship with the Church wasn't exclusively through me. In consulting and co-operating with my priest colleague, a healed priesthood was apparent.

A Pastoral Worker colleague in a psychiatric hospital was in close contact with a woman who had been there for four years and was now seriously ill. She had maintained good contacts with people in her home parish. The Pastoral Worker discussed with her parish priest how best to help her. Together they prepared the sacrament of the Last Rites and then anointed her together. This collaboration was beneficial for the patient, her family and friends, as well as staff and patients; the woman's life in the village and hospital belonged together and were healed.

Healing priesthood is characteristically holistic – a word of our time. In using it, I want to draw attention to the diverse aspects of life that are at the same time part of the whole. This means being accepted with 'all your baggage'. For me, it is clear that healing priesthood is only possible when it is integral to everyday life – not separate, an alien element. On the one hand, this calls for opportunities for priests to be sacramentally close to people in everyday life, without being overwhelmed by other work. On the other, it is a plea that Pastoral Workers, who are in close contact with people, be given the opportunity of confirming this contact in the administering of sacraments.

I dream of a priesthood which foregrounds the human dimension, on which different cultures may leave their mark, where both feminine and masculine have a place. Such a priesthood offers many opportunities for identification, connections and points of contact. Such a priesthood shows God's richness, revealing unexpected, sometimes hidden aspects. Such a priesthood is an invitation to many very different people to develop into healed human beings.

Note

1. In Dutch there is a play of words: *helen* meaning 'to heal', and *heel maken* meaning 'make whole/complete'.

KNEADING THE BREAD OF PRIESTHOOD

PAULINE O'REGAN rsm

The same day I sat down to begin this writing, I read a letter from a New Zealand nun in Peru. She wrote: 'We facilitate a pastoral centre here among a priestly people in a priestless parish. Our *parroquia* consists of forty isolated villages ... no priest or other religious. Wonderful, salt of the earth catechists act as leaders and celebrants in their communities.'[1] I knew immediately that here was the authentic setting for a *healed priesthood*. The Peruvian picture, as I see it, is made whole when the ordained priest comes to this 'priestly people' and the healing process would be complete if it were one of those 'wonderful, salt of the earth catechists' who became their ordained leader.

There can be little doubt that the clerical priesthood is suffering from a deep-seated malaise, but it is a sickness that cannot be healed in isolation. It cannot be healed, for instance, simply by changing laws in such matters as celibacy or by better psychological testing of seminarians, or any other treatment of visible symptoms. It is the body as a whole that is in deep trouble. It is the system that is sick. (It has to be said in passing that it is nothing short of a miracle of God's grace that so many manage to live healthy, functional lives within such a dysfunctional body.) The need for healing the priesthood does not lie primarily in its social and psychological ills. It goes much deeper. It has to do with theology – and specifically with the theology of priesthood that has been harboured and taught over generations.

As we see people of integrity in our communities walking away from the Church, as we see more and more women being alienated and as we see the ordained priesthood itself in increasing disarray, we know that our options are running out. This is especially true of the ordained priesthood, as we watch it slide downhill into the worldliness of clericalism. The attributes of clericalism: control, secrecy, abuse of power, fear of (if not contempt for) women, a cult of maleness – these are no part of the priesthood of Christ conferred on every Christian – male and female – at baptism, and given in its fullness to every ordained priest at Holy Orders.

Until the Second Vatican Council, we were taught a theology of baptism that was so limited as to be seriously distorted. For one thing, no emphasis was ever given to the fact that the primary call to the Christian through baptism is to share in the priesthood of Christ through the various gifts given by the Holy Spirit. Until the Council, the only understanding we had of priesthood was that conferred by Holy Orders. It wasn't that we didn't hear the words said in baptism, it was just that no one suggested we take them seriously: 'As Christ was anointed Priest, Prophet and King, so may you live also as members of his Body ...'[2] – and in the 'Introduction to the Rite of Christian Initiation': 'The anointing with chrism after Baptism is a sign of the royal priesthood of the baptised.'[3]

Women and men are increasingly aware that they have this priestly calling by right of baptism and that, in collaboration with the ordained priest, they are responsible for the spiritual and material well-being of Christ's Body on earth. No less an authority than Godfrey Diekmann, reviewing the Second Vatican Council, has noted that 'the greatest achievement of the Council was restoration of the baptismal dignity of the laity'.[4]

We seldom realise the role that language plays in moulding our thinking. We would go a long way towards good theological thinking in this matter of priesthood, if we made what many of us have discovered is a simple adjustment, easily acquired with practice. In our community, we have stopped speaking of 'the priest' as though there were only one priest and we say instead 'the ordained priest'. That leaves us free to speak of a 'priestly people'. The letter from Peru would then have read, 'a priestly people without an ordained priest'. There can, in truth, be no such thing as a 'priestless parish'.

We are not speaking of two priesthoods, but of the one priesthood of Christ, which we share in different degrees. This more careful use of language brings home to us that the ordained priest did not become a priest at Holy Orders. He became a priest at his baptism. He is a priest who is ordained. Holy Orders conferred on him the fullness of priesthood, to empower him to carry out the mission of the ordained priest, which is to minister to the people of God. To that end, he received the priestly power to celebrate the Eucharist, to minister the sacraments and to follow the model of leadership set by Jesus himself. His mission is to provide spiritual food for the people and to care for them with pastoral tenderness, so that they in their turn have the strength to carry out their particular mission of bringing Christ to the world in which they live and work.

I have not a single doubt that until the Church embraces fully, in practice as well as in word, its own teaching about the priesthood conferred on men and women through baptism, we will never have a proper appreciation of Holy Orders – and until it admits the justice, if not the simple logic, of extending to women the fullness of their priesthood, all talk of *healing priesthood* is doomed to failure.

It is imperative that theology be lifted off the page and applied in practice in this matter. If not, we will be left, not with the bread of priesthood, but with the stone of clericalism and its inevitable and equally destructive offspring – anti-clericalism.

God grant that we all become a part of *healing priesthood*. It is the Church of the future that is at stake.

Notes

1. *The Common Good*, Pentecost 2002 Correspondence Column, Christchurch, New Zealand.
2. 'Baptism of Children' in *The Rites of the Catholic Church as Revised by the Second Vatican Council* (New York), p. 208.
3. *ibid.*, 'Introduction to the Rite of Adult Christian Initiation', p. 28.
4. *Religious Life Review* (Dublin, March/April 1999), p. 118.

THE CHALLENGE OF HEALING

PETRONILLA SAMURIWO

Healing priesthood is indeed an ambiguous topic; therefore it is important not to take it out of context – the Church in the wider society, facing the myriad challenges of life in the twenty-first century.

Many priests I know and have worked with in Zimbabwe are wonderful people who demonstrate deep commitment to their work and are focused in their role as mediators between God and humanity, and in offering public prayers in the name of human society. I have also known priests who seem over-whelmed by the responsibilities invested in them, with often nasty and unpleasant consequences.

For some time, I have wondered why church leaders have a gripping fear of the media – this crucial instrument of communi-cation, which could be used in the whole process of healing. It seems to me that the media – secular, religious or otherwise – whether print, broadcast, theatre, etc., actually present many windows of opportunity in understanding the depths of problems within the Church.

For example, rather than being concerned about 'bad publicity' from the media, or trying to hide the extent of truth in allegations of abuse and other corruption, perhaps church leadership might want to consider the benefits of using various channels, including the media, to get dialogue going on how, as a Christian community, we can right the shameful wrongs in our history, past and present. How did we, for instance, get to a stage that sees nuns pressured into sexual relations with priests in return for 'necessary certificates and/or recommendations'?[1] Instead of recoiling into Catholic shells of conservatism, the Church in its entirety – lay people, religious and ordained – is challenged to make a concerted effort to deal with the issues that make us uncomfortable. Let's open up and talk about it. I see this as the crucial first step towards the process of healing. Action should not just be left to the Church's appointed leaders, as the entire Church has the obligation to be involved.

Closely linked to *healing priesthood* is the issue of gender and power relations within the Church. As in other parts of the world, Catholics in Africa are increasingly suffering from painful revelations about the ugly side of the Church. Over the years, we have read or listened in shock to stories in the media or through the traditional 'grapevine' about abusive priests who have used their office in unorthodox ways. Double standards are evident in the manner in which reprimands are made. According to Sister Maura O'Donoghue in her devastating report on clerical sexual abuse:

> When a sister becomes pregnant, she must leave her con-gregation, while the priest involved with her can continue his ministry . . . Some priests are recommending that sisters take contraceptives, misleading them that 'the pill' will pre-vent transmission of HIV. Others have actually encouraged abortion . . . Some priests are known to have relations with several women, and also to have children from more than one liaison . . .'[2]

In 2001, the Vatican acknowledged the sexual abuse of nuns by some priests and missionaries.

My resignation 'in protest' early last year from my post as editor of *Catholic Church New*s (a bimonthly magazine published by the Zimbabwe Catholic Bishops' Conference) resulted from my including an account of Sr Maura's report in the paper. As an editor appointed to make sober decisions in a positive, truthful approach to the newsworthiness of editorial content, I had not banked on the fact that the bishops for whom I worked could ban the sale of their own publication, merely because it contained some embarrassing truths about some members of the clergy. This went against everything I believed in professionally as a journalist, and spiritually as a Catholic. As a result, I terminated my employment with the Church. Spiritually I was shaken, but with hindsight I consider the event a good learning experience, which serves to remind me of the need for the Catholic Church to address proactively the grave issue of healing, not only of priesthood, but the entire Church.

Another opportunity for healing could be an in-depth analysis of the gender dynamics within the Church. Power, leadership and (importantly) decision-making remain the domain of men. There still remain gross inequalities in gender roles – *power to* and *power over*? For example, many people who are abused are women and children who submit to sexual advances out of obligatory condescension to the important role of the priest.

But we cannot merely talk about healing priesthood in isolation: we need to remember that our priests are also products of the larger community, raised in our families and socialised according to our local cultures and traditions. If society pressures a priest to prove virility by having children, then can we not say that the said community also needs some healing? In Africa, priests still have control of their own lives, can use resources for their own benefit, and even make reproductive decisions. Some people have suggested that the number of priests with children is much higher than currently envisaged. The number of priests thought to be dying of AIDS is also of concern. In Zimbabwe as a whole, it is estimated that 25 per cent of people between the ages of twenty-five and forty-five are infected with HIV. If 3 million of Zimbabwe's 12 million national population are estimated to be infected, then what of the future of male priesthood in Zimbabwe? HIV/AIDS is not only a public health and development problem, it also raises religious questions. The reversal of gains in life expectancy in Zimbabwe, now down to forty-six from fifty-four in 1992, also mirrors the reversal of gains in Christianity.

I have tried to outline here some of the challenges faced by the Church today and areas where I believe it is in need of healing. This is the context from which I come and in which I live; these are the challenges the Church can no longer afford to ignore.

Notes
1. Sr M. O'Donoghue, Report, see *National Catholic Reporter* website: www.natcath.com.
2. *ibid.*

THE PRIEST, COLLABORATION, AND SPIRITUAL LEADERSHIP

SHEILA GARCIA

One can sympathise with the cleric who, on his way to the US bishops' meeting to discuss sex abuse, stopped to exchange his collar for a sports shirt. Clerical travellers in mufti have undoubtedly increased as the image of the priesthood has declined. Not surprisingly, researchers at the Catholic University of America found that 62 per cent of a cross-section of US priests would like to see 'the image and esteem of the priesthood' more openly discussed.[1]

The sex abuse scandals provide a clue to addressing the theme *healing priesthood*. Let me identify two lessons from this crisis and then offer a model that responds to what we have learned.

Americans, whether Catholic or not, reacted with shock and outrage as charges of sexual misconduct and cover-ups surfaced in the Boston Archdiocese and spread to dioceses throughout the US. This reaction taught us lesson one: Catholics expect their priests and bishops to be the spiritual and moral leaders of the faith-community and, often, civil society. Like all leaders, they are held to standards of behaviour that reflect the trust and respect accorded to those in leadership positions. As spiritual leaders, they are expected to strive towards virtue, to be men whose deeds and words proclaim the presence of God among us.

The sense of betrayal generated by the scandals revealed how tightly we cling to this image of priest as spiritual and moral leader. It also showed our ambiguity about the image. We acknowledge a priest's normal human failings but are surprised when these shortcomings are revealed. As one lay Catholic wrote, 'I expected and wanted priests to be just like me, except better in every way that mattered.'[2]

The scandals provide a second lesson: a closed clerical culture isolates bishops and priests from each other and from the faithful. While the sexual misconduct of a few priests appalled American Catholics, the cover-ups by some bishops left them aghast. Here was spiritual leadership at its worst, exercised in an authoritarian, individualistic manner, with no attempt to consult the laity or to hear victims' stories.

While the scandals revealed the devastating effects of this closed culture, many American lay people, especially women, had already identified it as a major obstacle to the exercise of spiritual leadership. In 2001, the US Bishops' Committee on Women in Society and in the Church sponsored a consultation with women who hold diocesan leadership positions. Many participants spoke of their exclusion from church decision-making processes. They noted an excessive concern with power and authority on the part of some priests, especially the newly ordained, and an unwillingness, perhaps inability, to work with women. In short, the closed clerical culture produced priests who lacked the necessary attributes of genuine spiritual leadership.

Can we offer a model that responds to these concerns? Yes. Collaboration envisions the working together of all the baptised, each contributing specific gifts for the good of the Church. We know that collaboration benefits the laity, since it gives them a voice in church decision-making and allows their gifts and experiences to be used. But collaboration also benefits the clergy. Specifically, I contend that collaboration enables the priest's spiritual leadership to flourish. What helps the laity helps the clergy and, most importantly, helps the Church to accomplish Christ's mission in the world.

Let me identify five ways in which collaboration helps the

priest to become an effective spiritual leader.

First, collaboration requires role clarification, which leads to an emphasis on the priest's spiritual leadership. Roles are based on authority of office, such as pastor or bishop, and on an individual's particular competence, knowledge, and gifts. Although we may identify several roles for the priest (e.g. counsellor, administrator), most would agree that his sacramental role is primary. In the Catholic University survey, 90 per cent of priests said that administering the sacraments and presiding at liturgy was of greatest importance to them.[3] Laity agree on its significance; few question the priest's leadership role in the church's sacramental life, even as lay people participate more actively in liturgical celebrations.

The priest's sacramental role is the basis for his role as spiritual leader. We cannot expect perfection from those who lead us in worship, but we can expect an honest effort to imitate the one who is worshipped. We expect a certain holiness that marks the priest as spiritual leader. When the priest's role as sacramental minister is clarified and highlighted, as in collaborative ministry, then the priest's role as spiritual leader inevitably comes to the fore.

Second, a priest who works collaboratively comes to know and call forth people's gifts. Like Jesus, he exercises leadership by engaging the people. The collaborative priest passes the test of spiritual leadership, encouraging and enabling people to use their gifts for the good of society and the church. As one collaborative pastor wrote: 'The pastor's spiritual care is most often exercised through hiring and coaching good people, caring for the systems of the parish and having the time to think about and preach about the big picture of the parish's work for the Gospel.'[4] Because this pastor identifies and uses the gifts of others, he has time for the *personal touch* that he alone can give.

Third, leaders are judged by the decisions they make, and collaboration improves the quality of decision-making. Even the best spiritual leader lacks sufficient knowledge, wisdom and experience to make right decisions all the time. Collaboration gives access to what he lacks. Again, the sex abuse scandals are instructive. Had some bishops regularly sought the advice of parents, and then chosen to protect children rather than abusive priests, the scandals might never have happened.

Fourth, collaboration provides a way to ensure mutual accountability. This is important, since a perceived lack of accountability on the part of some priests and bishops has eroded their claim to spiritual leadership. When priests work collaboratively, they send a strong message about the responsible use of authority. They acknowledge that authority is God's gift, to be exercised for the common good, not a possession to be used for personal gain. In holding themselves accountable both to God and to the faith-community, they show humility consistent with spiritual leadership.

Finally, collaboration gives rise to healthy relationships that support the priest. Wise priests acknowledge their need for professional colleagues and personal friends who understand their burdens and lend encouragement. Collaboration is a seedbed for such relationships. It helps to counter the loneliness and burnout that afflict too many fine priests.

A renewed appreciation of the priest as spiritual leader, and how collaboration enhances that role, benefits the whole Church. For example, we can expect to see more lay leadership, as collaborative priests foster the gifts of lay men and women. Collaboration does not create winners and losers; it does not favour one group at the expense of another. It can heal a wounded priesthood; it can help priests to heal a wounded Church and society.

Notes

1. *The CARA Report*, Spring 2002, Centre for Applied Research in the Apostolate, Georgetown University, Washington, DC.
2. *America*, 6 May 2002, Mgr Vincent Rush: letter to the Editor.
3. *The CARA Report*, p. 11.
4. *The CARA Report*, p. 6.

MAUN ALIN IHA KRISTU[1]

MARIA LOURDES MARTINS CRUZ (MANA LOU)
in interview with
CATHERINE SCOTT

Mana Lou's order was not initially well understood by those who should have understood it best – the local hierarchy. Some clergy regarded her as a nuisance – a nun 'trying to be a priest'. It took a peace prize from Pax Christi International in 1996 for the East Timorese Church to wake up to the jewel in their midst. Gradually, hostility has waned. Mana Lou today is involved with priestly formation. Young seminarians are sent to her centre in the countryside of Dare to experience her work with the poor, travelling with her young novices for two weeks' pastoral work in remote areas, then reflecting on their experience – a chance to discuss faith and commitment and benefit from Mana Lou's unique spiritual direction.

If someone has a calling, asserts Mana Lou, she should answer to 'the reality of the people'. Like Moses and St Paul, we have to adapt and follow God's lead. If people respond to their society's needs, they are also responding to God and can thus develop spiritual life and, through prayer, become a friend of Jesus – meet him in the gospel: 'We see that Jesus was very simple,' says Mana Lou, 'and impassioned – always ready to act ... I sometimes get the impression that we Christians don't know who Jesus is. Social status becomes more important.

'I do not believe that vocations are just for men. We are all called to do something. I became a secular sister because I wanted to be compatible with the secular priests – they seem

111

happy with our role in the Church; we generally have a good relationship with them. We must give a good example, living as in basic Christian communities.

'Here in Dare we come together in community, to do something with our gifts – and we give moral support to each other. As women in the Church we start with real life. We try to understand the "why". When we study the Scriptures, we notice those who are most courageous: women are the first not to be afraid – women were first at the tomb. For a priest, saying Mass is easy, but to have an open heart to love and serve, especially for an educated person, that is very hard. We must be creative – I encourage girls here to understand the problems – talk by all means, but then act – open the gospel to people. And women here are getting involved creatively with liturgy – holding paraliturgies and so on.

The priesthood in East Timor started with Portuguese religious missionaries four centuries ago. During the Japanese occupation, the missionaries left, but have since returned. Nowadays, we have secular clergy as well. Seminary education here is very closed. There doesn't seem to be any thinking about the nature of God. We all need our own experience of God. Not just theology.'

That's where the experience with Mana Lou becomes formative 'The week before we go to the village,' she explains, 'we prepare. We study health issues, prepare traditional medicines, catechetical material, liturgies, and also for a counselling role. The young priests like these visits because, they say, "the people respect us. Yet they criticise us too!!" But to crave respect is poor motivation; as priests, they are also there to serve. In Timor, town priests just say Mass; there is not so much work for a priest. They may manage to be superficially "busy", but the work is no challenge to their commitment.

'Western culture is very open. Here a great deal is hidden, especially within the Church. This means that, as elsewhere, injustices do happen. We have our share of women being impregnated by priests and then brushed aside because the system cannot deal with them. Priests are not encouraged to take responsibility for this kind of misdemeanour. But they must. Individuals should be respected, but the Church will have to democratise here.

'Priests should be in a good position to understand women. And my experience is that most of them *do* – apart from the arrogant ones, who cannot see beyond their own criticisms.

'I believe that whether a priest or a sister, you have to have a "male and female" heart. I mean by this that you need to have a profound understanding and empathy with both men and women. We have to understand each other across the gender divide. God is our Father and our Mother – that is why humanity is mixed. When men talk to me, I understand them with my "male side". I have this as well as the feminine. God calls us to serve many people. If I am a woman and I only attend to women, I would be in trouble. Sometimes there is trouble in the Christian family because people only think of themselves.

'Women have so much to contribute. Priests love to stay in Dare because here the church is home too – not just a building. They come to realise that their barren presbyteries are miserable places by comparison. Even my cousin, who is a priest, has learned from us in that respect, and opened his house up a little. Sometimes priests are imprisoned by their so-called spirituality. Here we encourage them to have a relationship with us.

'In the beginning, when I was setting up this place, I had problems. I was the first laywoman to start something. People did not understand why we did not behave like other sisters. We began by organising free clinics for the poor. We did not worry about having few resources – we just thought of the birds and lilies in Matthew's Gospel. We knew that God would not abandon us. Now we have a bank account, lots of people want to help us, and we are starting to do micro-credit projects in some of the villages. But we don't worry about money. When it comes – good – we'll put it to good use. Some students from

Melbourne gave us a truck. People have come to help organise handicraft production, organic crops, rice. We're thinking about how to develop East Timorese culture. Another donor gave us a big tractor, but it broke down and we can't get the spare parts to fix it. I am sometimes sceptical of all these NGOs.[2] The worst ones objectify our suffering – that is horrible.'

Indeed, Mana Lou has built up a healthy scepticism about NGOs and 'Projects'. She is more interested in sharing skills and teaching people practical things that they can do for themselves. Recently the centre has been getting into soap and shampoo manufacture out of local ingredients.

When I asked whether she would have liked to be a priest, Mana Lou shrugged. Clearly the question had never consumed her. 'I prefer to be itinerant and travel around,' she said.

Notes

1. Brothers and Sisters in Christ.
2. Non-governmental organisations, many of which besieged East Timor, 2000–02.

A SYROPHOENICIAN WOMAN'S
SHARE IN JESUS'
PRIESTLY MINISTRY[1]

TERESA OKURE SHCJ

The title above may come as a double shock to the Catholic
reader. First, women have no priestly ministry, except a share in
the nebulous ordinary 'priesthood of the baptised'. Second, if
even Catholic women can have no share in Jesus' priesthood on
the basis of their God-given sex, how then can a pagan woman
of the first century AD, in Jesus' own lifetime, be perceived as
sharing in this ministry? Yet John Paul II, in *Novo Millennio
Ineunte*, invites us to summon up courage to 'launch into the
deep' and abandon those cumulate 'deviations from the gospel'
that crept in during the past two millennia.[2]

The qualities of Jesus' priesthood, as recorded especially in
Hebrews, include solidarity with us in suffering unto death and
resurrection ('like us in all things but sin'); the sacrifice of himself to destroy in his person all barriers that stood in the way of
union between God and human beings and among humans
themselves; and, now that he is in heaven, powerful and cease-
less intercession. In the Catholic tradition, certain priests are
also given the faculties to act as exorcists or cast out demons.
Jesus' priesthood then is essentially about compassion (suffering
with), liberation from oppressive forces, healing and wholeness.
One shares in this priesthood by performing any of these
priestly functions.

How does this apply to the Syrophoenician woman? Mark
presents her as a pagan woman of mixed blood ('a Greek, a

Syrophoenician by birth'). She goes directly to Jesus, breaking the cultural taboo by which women did not speak to men in public, and acting against Jesus' own wish to remain hidden in the region. Though uncharacteristically the disciples here seem to show sympathy for the woman ('Give her what she wants' [Matt.]), their real concern is to save themselves from the embarrassment of her 'crying after us'. Uncharacteristically too, Jesus seems to take the hard line of ignoring her, citing the divine restriction on his mission: 'I was sent only to the lost sheep of the house of Israel'. The woman thus has no biological, racial or religious right to approach Jesus. But as a mother, she has the right to seek to rid her little girl of 'severe' demon possession. This duty is also divinely entrusted to her as a woman and mother. No human authority can nullify it. Her love and compassion for her little girl (her suffering with her, as Jesus, God's high priest, suffered with humanity), leads her to ignore the cultural prohibitions and transcend the racial barrier that even Jesus here seems to endorse.

When the woman reaches him, Jesus rubs it in even harder by telling her proverbially, 'It is not right to take the children's bread and throw it to pet house dogs', advising that she should, 'Let the children be fed first'. He thus lays on the woman the responsibility of knowing and doing what is right. His treatment of her recalls that of his mother in John 2: 'My hour has not yet come'. Like Mary, this woman refuses to accept Jesus' position and replies, 'Yes, Sir, yet even house dogs eat the crumbs that fall from their master's table'. Put differently, she is not interested in taking away the children's food. Rather, she claims her own right to be fed, since (as a house dog) she too belongs as equally to the master as do the children. Jesus, therefore, cannot use the children's right to be fed to deprive her of her own right to be fed from the master's table.

As in Cana ('Do whatever he tells you'), so here, Jesus is beaten hands down by the woman's undaunted theological perception. In admiration he exclaims, 'Woman, great is your faith.

Because of this your word, go, the demon has left your daughter.' He does not say, 'I have cast the demon from your daughter', but, 'Because you have said this, the demon has left your daughter.' The power of her undaunted conviction of her right to belong has effected her daughter's cure. Her faith in Jesus and her mother's love confer on her the right to share in Jesus' priestly ministry of healing and exorcising demons. This recalls another woman priest-figure, also a Gentile, the widow of Zarephath, whom Jesus cites in his inaugural sermon in Nazareth (Luke 4): by God's design and her faith in God's word spoken through Elijah, she serves as God's agent in miraculously providing daily bread for Elijah, her little son and herself. Her ministry prefigures the Gospel miracles of the loaves and ultimately the Eucharist.

What can we learn from this story? Jesus allows a Gentile woman to invade his privacy and overrule what he perceived as the divine plan and will for him, just as he did in Cana. By being open to her priestly mediation and theologising, Jesus allows his own priestly ministry to be moved beyond the limits of racial exclusion to universal inclusiveness.

Like Jesus, the hierarchical Church needs to listen to women as they develop holistic and all-inclusive Christologies and sacramentology based solidly on the Scriptures, not on exclusivist, patriarchal traditions. They need to heed the persistent cries of women: it is not for men to use Jesus to send women away, since the priesthood is that of Jesus. Women, like men, belong equally to the Master as integral members of his body through their God-given birthright of baptism, whereby both women and men become new creatures and one indivisible person in Christ.[3]

Only by listening to women's voices and being open to, welcoming and celebrating women and their unique, God-given gifts of healing, will the priesthood itself be truly healed. Thus healed, it will be energised and empowered to cast out the many demons of our time, rooted mainly in patriarchy (militarism, terrorism, mammonism, abuse of power, fundamentalism, globalisation). It will be liberated from the bondage of maleness to which the Church has subjected it for almost two millennia, to serve as God's instrument for healing our demon-possessed and self-torturing world. Thus it will accomplish that for which Christ died and lives on, namely, the gathering into one of 'all God's scattered children' (John 11:52) irrespective of sex, race, colour or creed.

Notes
1. Mark 7:24–30; Matt. 15:21–28.
2. *Novo Millennio Ineunte*, no. 53.
3. See 2 Cor. 5:17; Gal. 3:28; 1 Cor. 12:13.

PRIESTHOOD AND COMMUNITY: THE FEMININE DIMENSION

VIRGINIA SALDHANA

As women, our reflection on Church has often centered on the ministerial priesthood. We have tried to understand its true meaning, expression, and service to the people. Often experiences shared indicate that the power enjoyed by priests in the Church is *power over* people rather than *power for* people.

When we talk of a *healing priesthood*, the image of *mother* comes to mind. The power she exercises is the power of love in nurturing, healing and holding the family together. Similarly, a healing priesthood is one that exercises power with love, where power is exercised with people to be in solidarity with them, understanding their pain and bringing wholeness.

Contrary to being a healer in the community, priests often hurt people and turn them away from the Church. Our society in India is deeply rooted in patriarchy. Most women accept their submissive role and status in the Church and society, though now some of the younger generation of women question this. In a society strongly rooted in patriarchy, we can hardly expect the qualities of love, gentleness and caring to be cultivated during priestly formation. One may find a few exceptions among priests who come from a background that has nurtured these qualities.

We have struggled to understand the exclusion of women from the ministerial priesthood and found no convincing theological explanation or scriptural basis for this exclusion. We have come to the unanimous conclusion that women seek a priesthood that is very different from the kind of priesthood that is exercised today.

Women understand priesthood as service, modelled on the priesthood of Jesus. God's love was made manifest in Jesus' dealings with people. His compassion, caring concern, and reaching out to bring healing and hope is similar to that expressed by persons with a feminist perspective. Women can more easily emulate the priesthood of Jesus because of the qualities of caring, nurturing, sacrificing and inner strength they have been encouraged to cultivate down the ages; precisely the qualities that are required for building people and community, but which are not encouraged in men brought up in a 'macho' patriarchal society.

More than ever, our world today needs a *healing priesthood*. People are subjected to a lot of stress and pressures from modern-day living. The economic situation puts great strain on families. Situations of conflict, local and international, add to the tensions within and between communities of peoples. Instead of attitudes of arrogance and superiority, we need gentle understanding, compassion and forgiveness to heal and sustain people.

In India, one finds women foremost in the areas of offering compassionate care, counselling, working for justice among the poor and marginalised, as catechists, and being with people in moments of need. The promotion of the small Christian community or basic community in the Church in Asia has developed women's leadership in the neighbourhood, which provides the feminine dimension in community building. This *common priesthood* expressed by women is vital for healing and holding communities together. But woman's contribution has to go beyond the sphere of the family and neighbourhood to bring healing and a wholeness to the Church and the world!

A REFLECTION

BISHOP VINCENT MALONE

Auxiliary Bishop of Liverpool and Episcopal Liason, NBCW

The word 'tradition' can sustain many meanings. Sometimes it is simply describing how our organisation (or family) has done things for the last few years. Sometimes it is used of a whole denomination of the Christian faith, seen as defined by the way it has long understood and practised the principles involved in the following of Christ. Specifically, the Catholic Church invokes divinely inspired *tradition* as the partner and interpreter of the written sacred Scriptures. That tradition is seen as graced with a normative role that guards from error, but may sometimes seem only to inhibit the freedom to engage with difficult questions.

Within any tradition it is a refined art to distinguish between what is at the heart of the principles it enshrines, and what is simply the current, perhaps variable, practice surrounding those principles.

The Catholic tradition, of which the Holy Father is the prime custodian, has within the present pontificate ruled that the ordination of women is not an area for creative exploration (which is not to say that it is unsuitable for humble reflection). But it has not so ruled in other areas which might yield surprising fruits.

Think, for instance, about the administration of the sacraments. The headline of the Catholic tradition might say, 'The administration of the sacraments is restricted to those in Holy Orders.' The smaller print might note the exception in the case of the sacrament of Matrimony, administered by the couple to each other. A footnote might add that the sacrament of baptism also can validly (and, in case of necessity, licitly) be administered by a lay person. But there are two other sacraments which Catholic discipline does not allow a lay man or woman to administer where the reason for the prohibition may not be immediately clear – the sacraments of Reconciliation and the Anointing of the Sick. Are these prohibitions of the essence of Catholic teaching, or merely the currently received practice?

It is a legitimate part of the answer to examine the history of the Church's practice, but a historical examination alone might not be conclusive. Within our own lifetime we have learned lessons that seem obvious in hindsight, however unthinkable they were before – about the use of Latin as the liturgical language of the Western Church, for instance, or the commissioning of lay women and men as ministers of the Eucharist. It's easy to accept now that there is no reason against such changes, but there have been times when the former practices seemed to be important elements of tradition.

So could the Church think of the possibility that a lay man or woman attending a sick person could not only pray with them and pray over them, but could pray the Church's most solemn prayers over them with sacramental anointing? Certainly no individual can simply take that initiative by himself/herself and act against the present discipline of the Church: that would not be a sacramental act. But could not the universal Church together reflect on the possibility that a lay person might administer this sacrament, as a wonderful focus of their already most welcome ministration of charity to one who needs to be 'raised up'?

And in the sacrament of Reconciliation, could not a lay person be seen by the Church, after prayerful reflection, as the authorised speaker of the forgiveness that comes in reality from God alone? It is not difficult to conceive circumstances in which a female minister could more appropriately than a man be the receiver of the humble confession that opens a soul to hear the glad words of the Lord's forgiveness.

Common practice in our society today would expect equal access in many professions to either a man or a woman at the client's choice. It would be an unusual medical group practice which did not have both male and female practitioners, similarly with a firm of solicitors or a team of counsellors. Has the time come to expect a similar availability in even more sacred areas of our lives – without thinking that this is impossible without the ordination of women?

Such thoughts are not intended as an incitement to rebellion; rather they are a quiet reflection on what is meant by *healing priesthood*. The ambiguous phrase may refer to a service that heals, and could perhaps do so more effectively; or to a service capable of being healed – being revisited in its immutable heart, so as to be clothed anew in the ever changeable vesture of the one High Priest, who chooses to reach out to us and to speak to us where we actually are.

AFTERWORD

The drawing together of these threads of insight and experience, so generously given by women worldwide in response to our invitation, shows many common elements although they come from a diversity of culture and background.

These women have committed themselves in various ways to living the Gospel in the service of the Church and the world, despite continuing struggles, pain, bewilderment and challenge to find co-responsible ways of being women in the Church. It is clear that their motivation is love for people and for the Church, and it is in that context that time and again the contributors call for compassion and understanding for ordained priests and for women – an example perhaps, of the 'ordinary life-giving healing ministry' suggested by Pia Buxton in her model of the Gossiping Church.

Abuse scandals have brought the ordained ministry and Church leadership into close scrutiny: 'here was spiritual leadership at its worst, exercised in an authoritarian, individualistic manner with no attempt to consult laity or hear victims' (Sheila Garcia). Consequently, lay people are questioning the use and mis-use of authority and leadership in the Church today.

In contrast, Pat Jones quotes John O'Donoghue, speaking of the ordained priesthood as existing 'to awaken and realize the implicit priestliness of each person'. Women here bear constant witness to the healing presence of that ministry and they affirm the specific place of the priest in the holy ordering of our parish communities. It is an important role demanding particular gifts and skills. Deeper discernment of the vocation to ordained ministry, a community-based system of seminary education, life-long formation, and good interpersonal skills are identified as crucial elements of a healing priesthood.

A significant theme is the challenge presented to the Church by the Second Vatican Council, particularly the teaching on the priesthood of the baptised. Pauline O'Regan reminds us of our 'primary call ...to share in the priesthood of Christ through the various gifts given by the Holy Spirit'. Growing awareness of the mission and ministry of the priesthood of the baptised alongside that of the ordained priest brings persistent calls for greater emphasis on collaborative ministry. Conversation and dialogue can lead to recognition of the need for change in perception and fresh understanding.

Language influences and reflects attitudes. Sr Patricia Howes describes the exclusive use of men, brothers and sons as 'contrary to the acceptance which opens us to the presence of Christ ... To be accepted, valued, included: these are gifts the Lord gave and which the priest can mediate, and something as simple as language can help or hinder this'. In *Healing Priesthood*, language is inclusive, affirming the validity of the feminine in everyone, and in our perception and understanding of God.

All the women's voices draw attention to the value for the Church as a whole – clergy and laity – of working together to explore nurturing, enabling models of power and leadership and to develop collaborative approaches to ministry and mission. This can only be achieved by walking alongside each other – sharing and receiving insight and knowledge in courageous conversation.

Angela Perkins and *Verena Wright*

NOTES ON CONTRIBUTORS
(in alphabetical order of Christian name)

Angela Harpham has worked as an appointed mental health chaplain, using the arts in spiritual awareness groups. With an MA (theology) and training in spiritual companioning, she is engaged in counselling, marriage preparation, and retreat-giving. Angela and Martin have been married for thirty-five years and parented three sons.

Anna Rowlands lives in North Wales with her husband (an Anglican priest), and their young son. She has worked in lay chaplaincy in special needs and mainstream education. She is currently completing a PhD in theology at the University of Manchester and has a particular interest in questions of religion, culture and gender.

Catharina Liduina Maria (Toos) Starman entered the Religious Congregation of the Ladies of Bethany (1956). She was trainer of catechesis teachers; pastoral worker in charge of a parish in Apeldoorn, a middle-sized town in the centre of the Netherlands (1976–98); and President of the Board of the Ladies of Bethany (1988–95).

Christine (Allen) Dench, Director of the Catholic Institute for International Relations (CIIR), has a degree in international relations and philosophy and an MSc in voluntary sector organisation. She has long experience of housing, poverty and social exclusion in the UK and maintains close contact with activity for peace and justice.

Ellen Teague, a freelance journalist and campaigner on justice,

127

peace and ecology issues, writes for *The Tablet, Messenger of St. Anthony* and Redemptorist Publications. She has edited *Vocation for Justice*, a Columban Missionary Society publication, for twelve years. She is married with three sons.

Geraldine Hawkes, the inaugural Chair of the Bishops' Commission for Australian Catholic Women, facilitates the greater participation of women in the Church in Australia. She is Co-ordinator of an ecumenical Centre for Ethics and was the laywoman on the leadership team for the Archdiocese of Adelaide.

Sr Joan Marshall is a religious of the Sisters of St Mary of Namur. During her thirty-five years in religious life she has spent five in the UK, seven in Africa and twenty-three in Brazil. Her apostolate was mostly catechetics and parish work. Her latest mission is serving as a General Councillor in the Congregation.

Kate Stogdon, a Cenacle Sister based in Manchester, has worked in the areas of spirituality and social justice for the last fourteen years. Currently she is studying for a doctorate focusing on the practice of 'self-surrender' in the light of feminist theology.

Kathryn Turner is editor of the Catholic diocesan newspaper *Portsmouth People* and an associate writer for the Redemptorists. She also designs and maintains the *Wellspring* website (www.wellsprings.org.uk) which offers liturgical and spiritual resources born from her work in parish and in leading workshops and days of reflection.

Sr Louise Swanston SSMN has a background in modern languages, theology and spirituality. She now lives in community in London. Ministries have included teaching, school chaplaincy, parish work and – her first love – retreats and spiritual accompaniment. Passions are linguistic, literary, musical and scriptural. She writes for *Bible Alive*.

Maria Lourdes Martins Cruz is the foundress of Maun Alin Iha Kristu, a secular institute based in Dare, East Timor. She trains young women to go and work and bear witness to the poorest of the poor in remote East Timorese villages, and to teach practical skills: health care, animal husbandry, etc. **Cathy Scott**, Joint Programme Manager for Asia who has managed CIIR East Timor project since 1991, interviewed Mana Lou, whom she first met in 1994.

Sr Mary Pia is a member of the Carmelite community at Golders Green, London. Born on the Pakistan/Afghan border, she grew up in the English Lake District, and became a Catholic while studying at Liverpool University. Her brother-in-law is a retired Anglican bishop, her sister-in-law a member of the Greek Orthodox Church, while her brothers hold no religious faith. She values her friendship with a young priest working in an inner-city parish.

Pat Jones is Deputy Director of CAFOD, the official development and humanitarian agency of the Catholic community in England and Wales. Previously she was Assistant General Secretary of the Bishops' Conference and has a background in theology, spirituality and adult education. She writes here in a personal capacity.

Patricia Howes is a Poor Clare Sister at Arundel, Sussex. At present she is Formation Director; amongst her other tasks are cooking and gardening.

Pauline O'Regan was born in New Zealand (1922). A Sister of Mercy, she taught history and was Principal for twenty years. With two sisters, Pauline pioneered the concept of living in a small community in a state-housing suburb, initiating community development and leadership training for local women. Her books include *A Changing Order*. She received a CBE for work in education and community (1990) and is a Distinguished Companion of the New Zealand Order of Merit (2001).

Petronilla Samuriwo, a journalist, human rights and HIV/AIDS activist in Zimbabwe, is a former editor of *Catholic Church News* (a bimonthly magazine of the Zimbabwe Bishops' Conference).

Pia Buxton joined the Institute of the Blessed Virgin Mary in the

1950s and taught for twenty years at St Mary's School, Ascot. She served as Novice mistress for nine years and as Provincial (1991–7), during which time she was President of the Conference of Religious (CoR). She currently works as a spiritual director and is Chair of the Catholic National Retreat Movement.

Rosemary Read works for the National Justice and Peace Network. Trained as a history teacher, she worked in Kenya and in a large Catholic comprehensive school in Derby. She has been a part-time parish assistant and worked in catechetics. Her justice and peace work has given her the opportunity to visit Central America, Southern Africa and Peru.

Sheila Garcia is Staff to the US Conference of Catholic Bishops' Standing Committee on Women in Society and in the Church. This comprises seven bishop-members and five women advisers. Recent initiatives have focused on domestic violence, women in Church leadership, collaboration between women and clergy, and women's spirituality in the workplace.

Teresa Okure SHCJ, a well-known biblical scholar, teaches Scripture at the Catholic Institute of West Africa, Port Harcourt, Nigeria.

Tina Beattie is a lecturer in Christian Studies at the University of Surrey Roehampton. She is a member of the NBCW Sub-Committee on Bioethics, and has written a number of books on theology and gender in the Catholic Church.

Vicky Cosstick has worked for the last fifteen years in adult education and formation of lay people, seminarians and clergy for many parishes, dioceses and national groups and organisations. She aims through her work to help build a collaborative, evangelising Church.

Virginia Saldhana is Co-ordinator of the Women's Committee of the Federation of Asian Bishops' Conferences.